Mega Doodle 2 Coloring Book

60 Fantastic Designs

For Coloring In.

By Artist
Dwyanna Stoltzfus

Join the Fun!!

Share your colored pages!!

You are invited to color the pages

From this and all publications by

Dwyanna Stoltzfus. Then scan and post

Your colored creations in

Coloring with Dwyanna

Adult Coloring Group

On facebook

https://web.facebook.com/groups/1519357628356169/?_rdr

Join Coloring with Dwyanna Coloring Group,

And have fun sharing your colored pages

And meeting new coloring friends.

Members of the group will also have access

To free coloring pages.

You are welcome to share your colored pages on

Any social network, make sure to mention the title of

The book and the author/artist name.

Uncolored images may not be shared.

Check out my blog at:

coloringwithdwyanna.blogspot.com

PDF Printable coloring pages available

On Etsy at

https://www.etsy.com/people/dwyannastoltzfus

Follow Dwyanna's art on facebook at

Oodles of Doodles Designs –

Adult Coloring Books by

Dwyanna Stoltzfus

https://web.facebook.com/Oodles-of-Doodles-Designs-Adult-Coloring-Books-by-

Dwyanna-Stoltzfus-743502922387046/

About:

Get ready to color 60 fantastic doodle art designs by Artist Dwyanna Stoltzfus.

In this adult coloring book you will find 60 fantastic illustrations, printed one per page.

A collection of wonderful images. In this book you will find a variety of .

Doodle art designs. Some with lots of detail and some with less detail.

There are some gorgeous floral designs, fantastic masks, kaleidoscope designs,

Mirrored designs and more!

You can use this coloring book to help you relax and unwind after a long day.

Or you can use it just for fun. You can color the designs simply or add depth

and creativity by shading and highlighting. Crayons are not recommended for the intricate

detail in this book but can be used on a few of the designs. You can color with fine tip markers,

gel pens, and colored pencils. Ultra fine tip markers and fine liners

work great on the designs that have intricate detail.

Enjoy the experience of coloring!!

But most of all relax and have fun!!

Coloring tips:

If you desire to add depth to your coloring you can shade with colored pencils.

Use dark colors around edges and into the peaks. Blend in light colors for the

middle and more open spaces. You can use black to darken areas,

and white to lighten and brighten areas.

Acknowledgments

Thank You to my family for all your support
of my art and this project.
I could not have done it without you!!

Thank You God for the gift and love
Of art and drawing!!

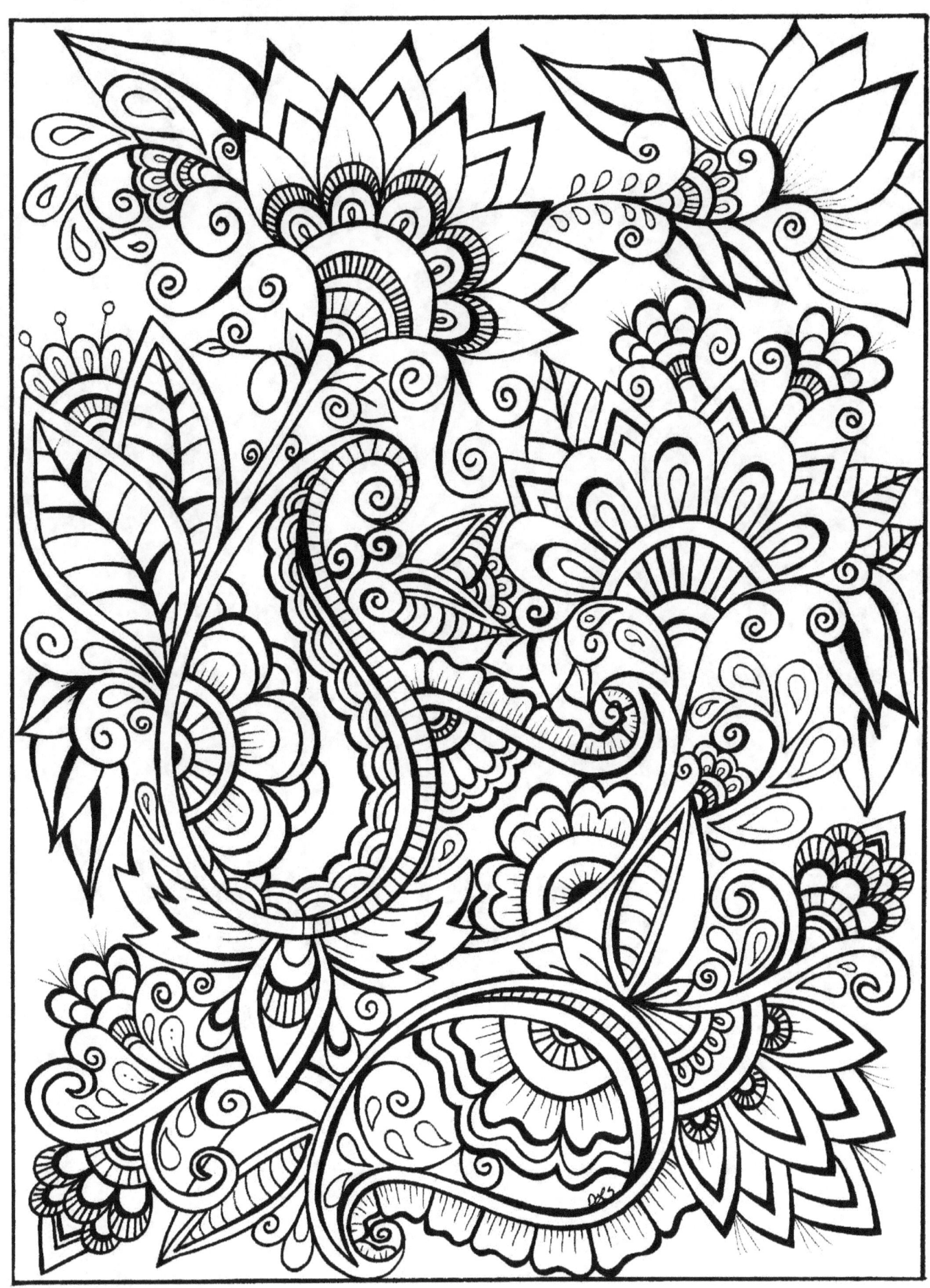

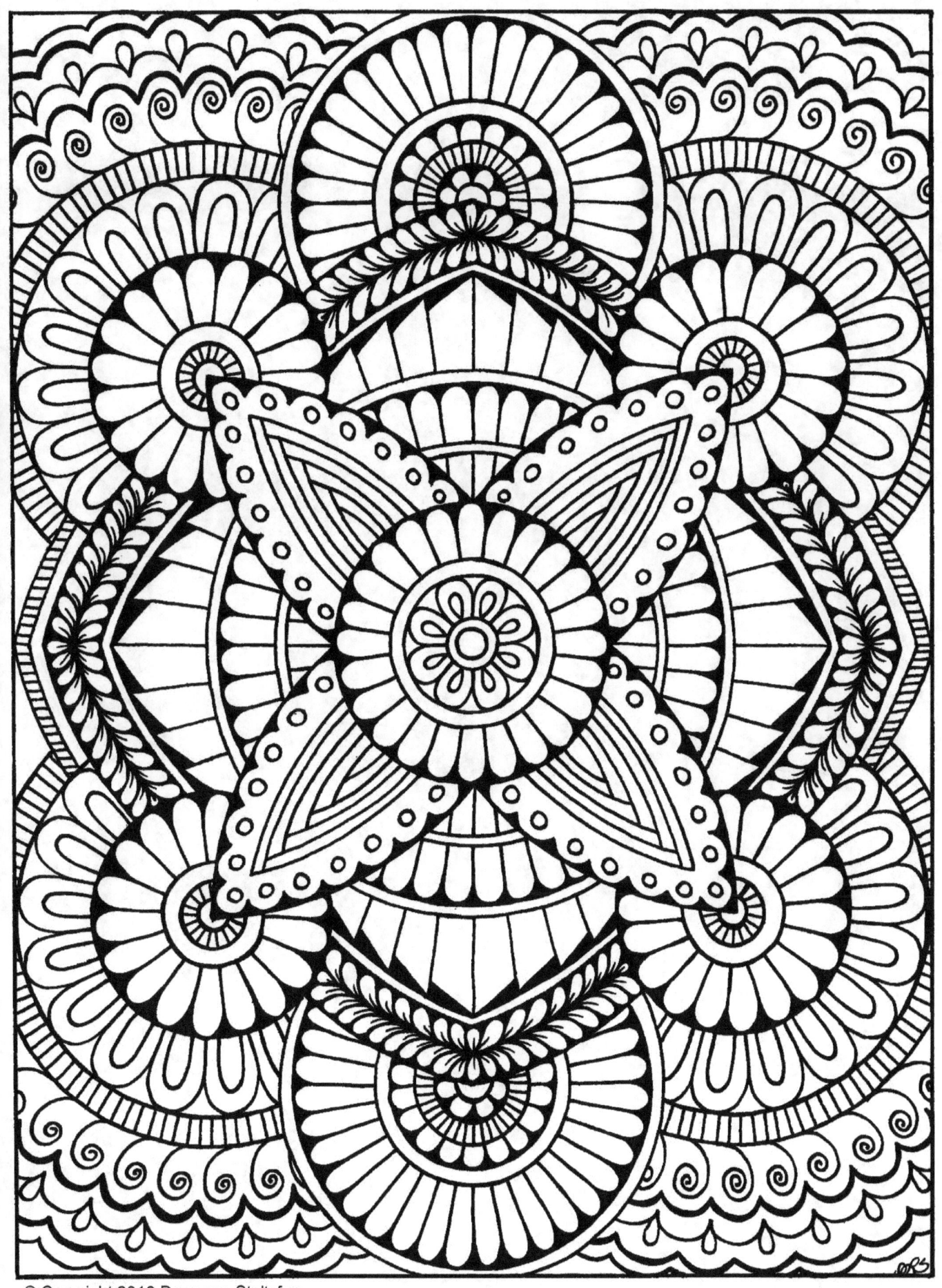

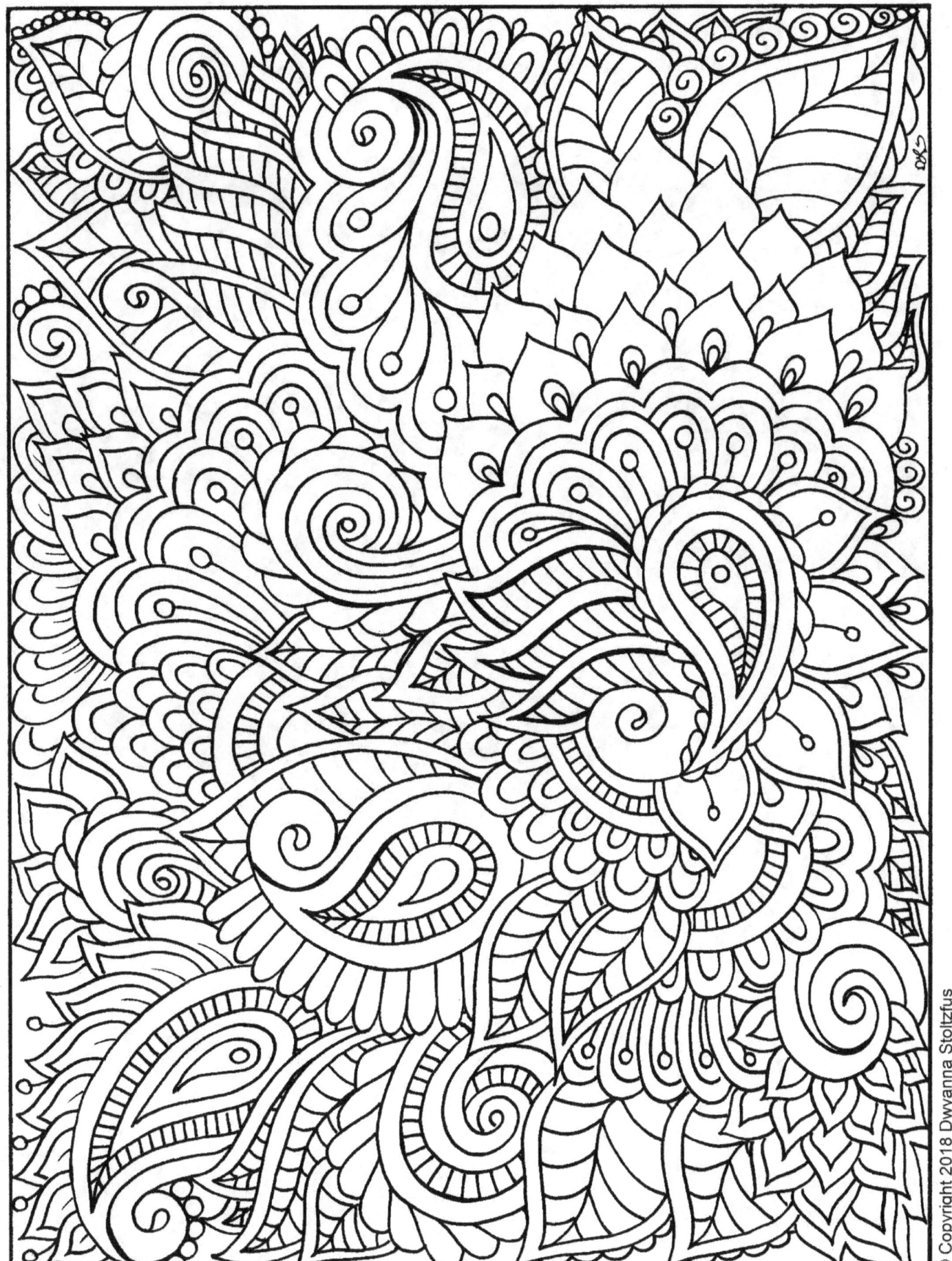

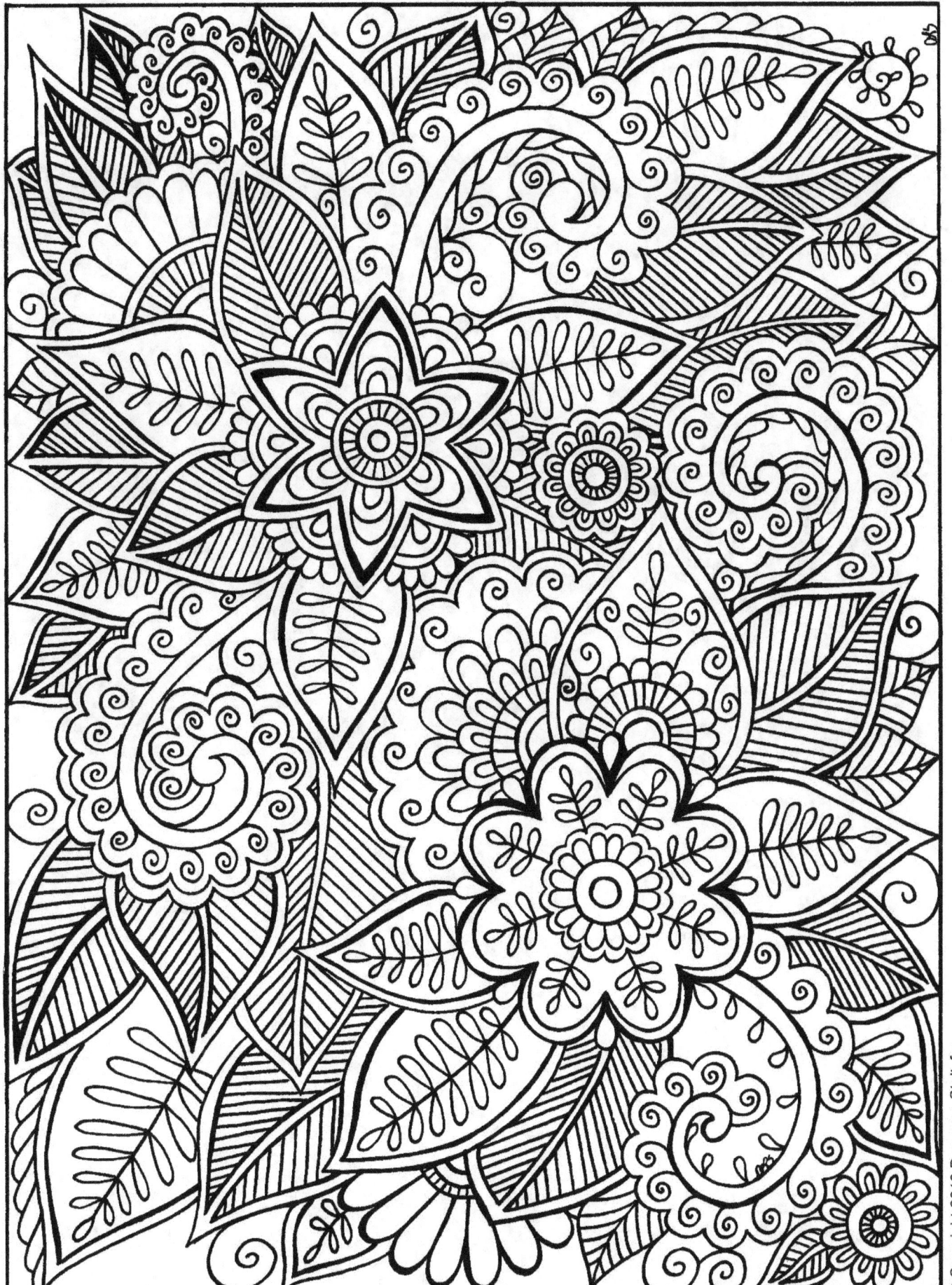

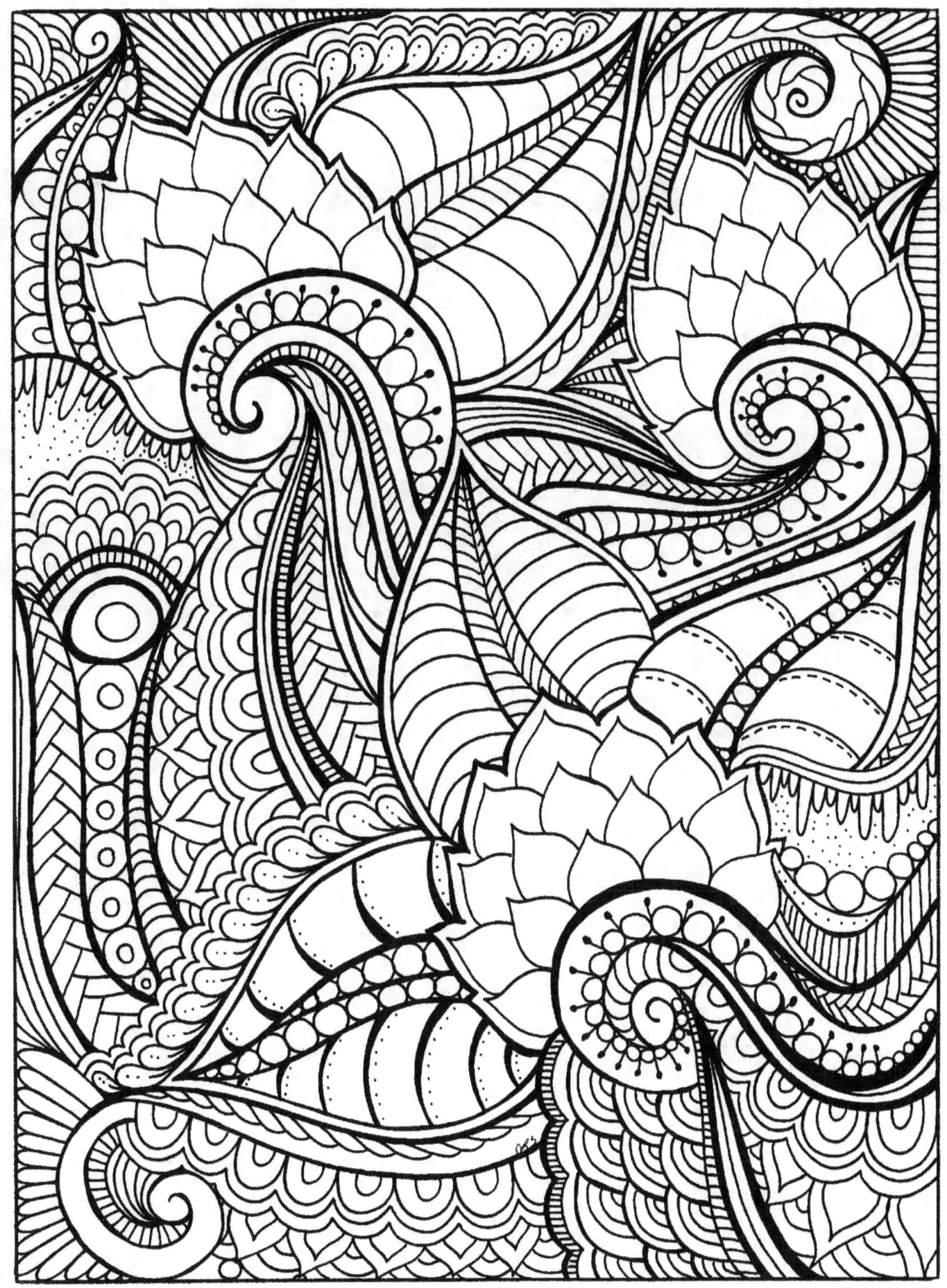

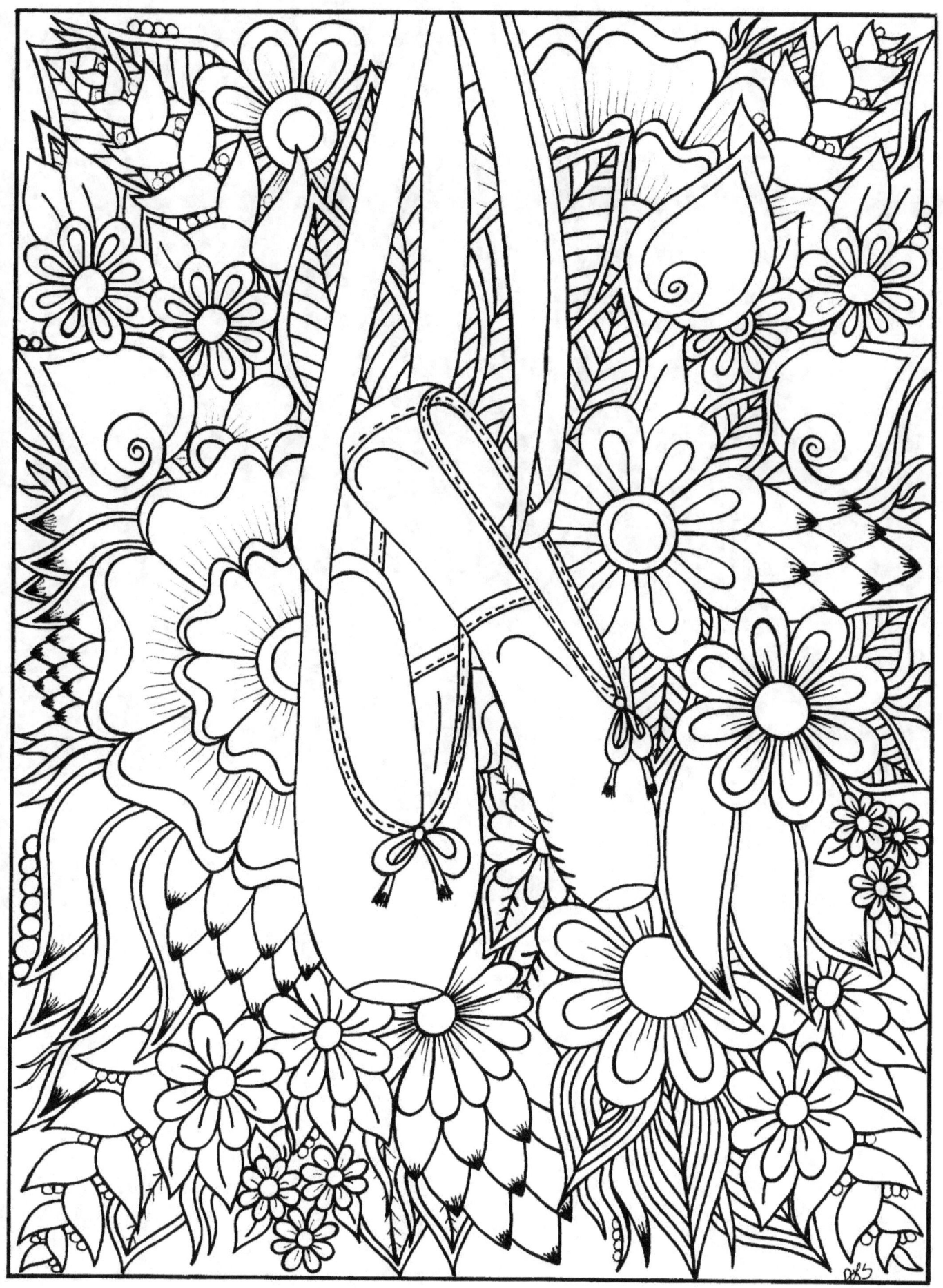

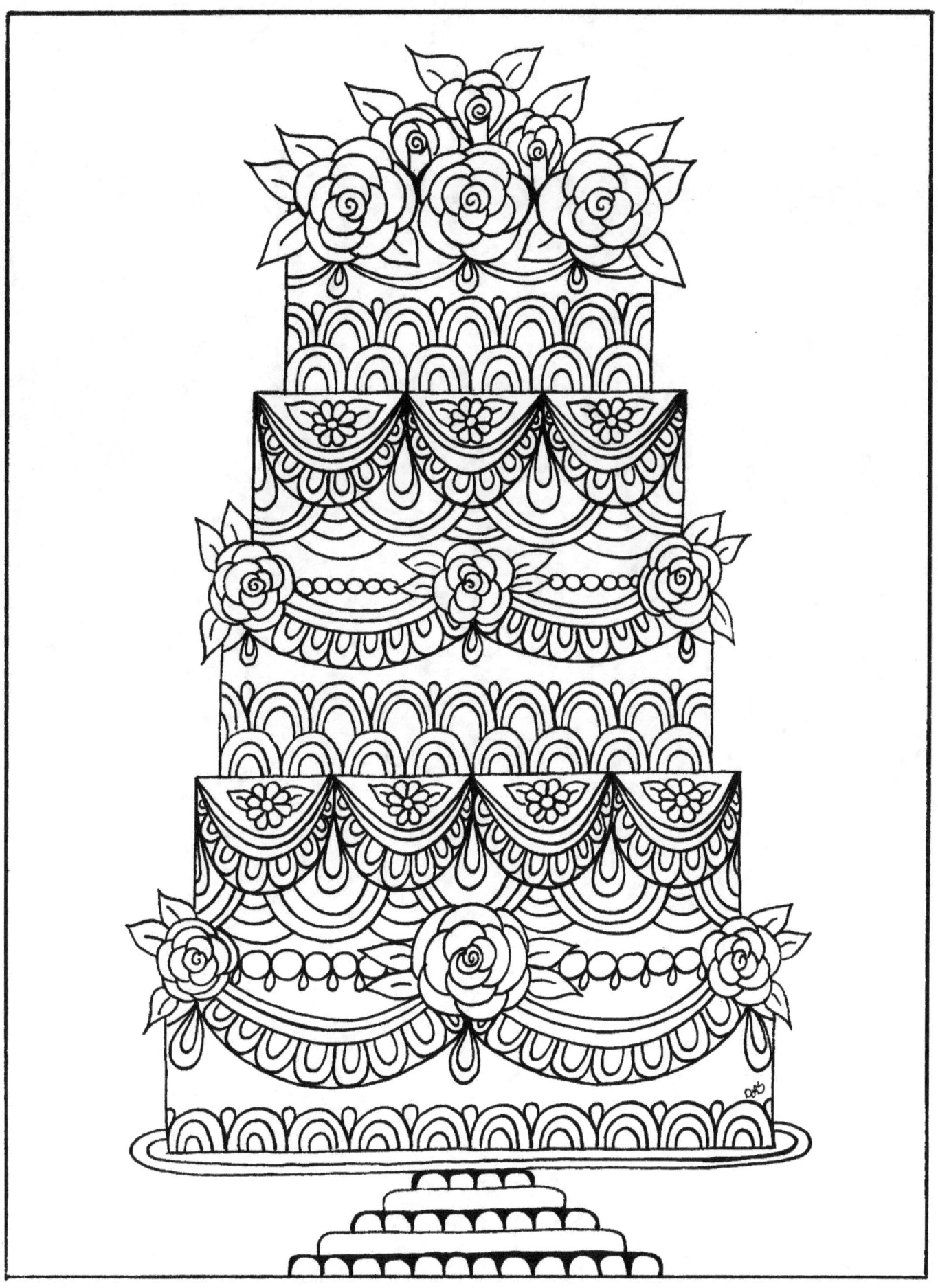

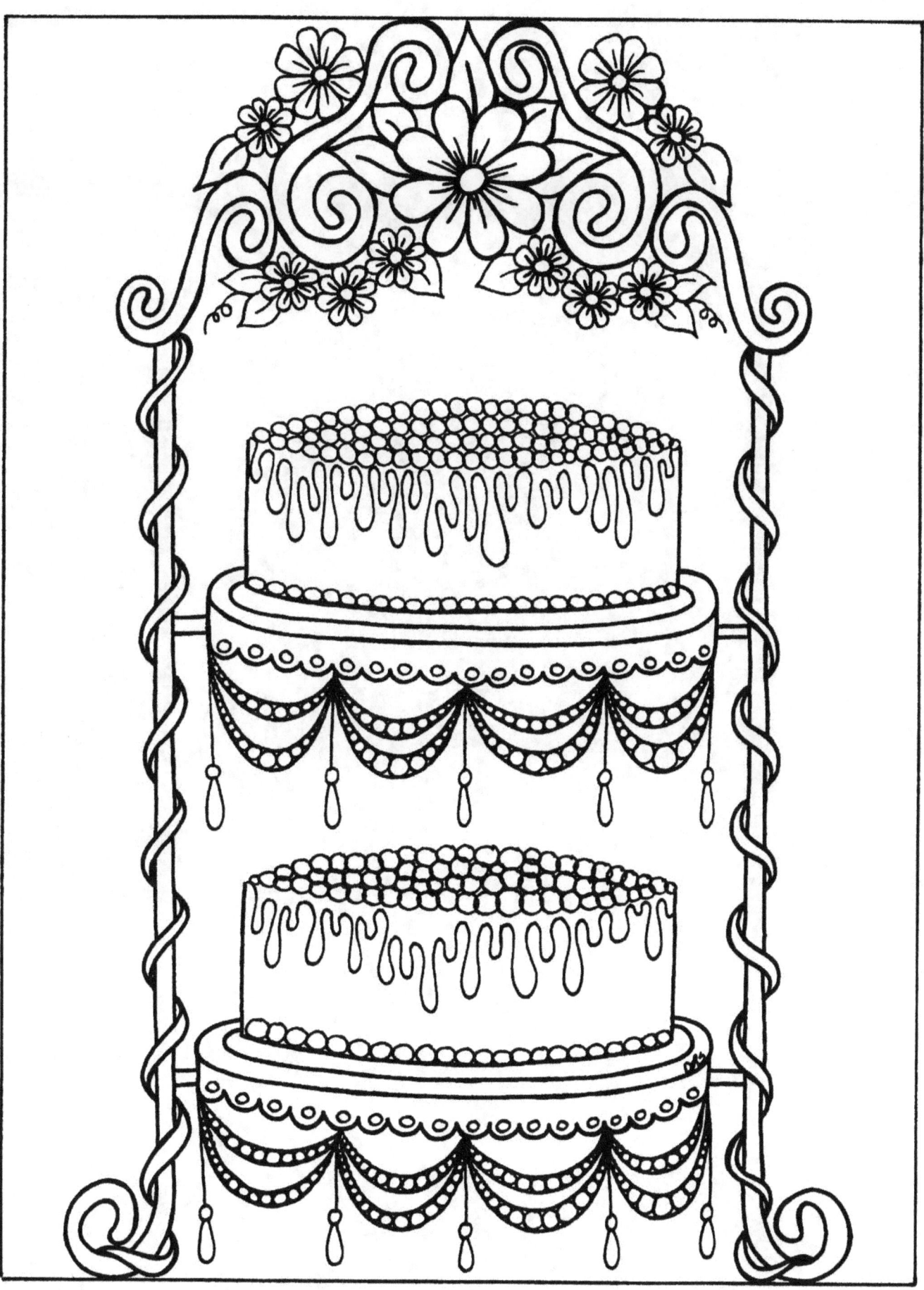

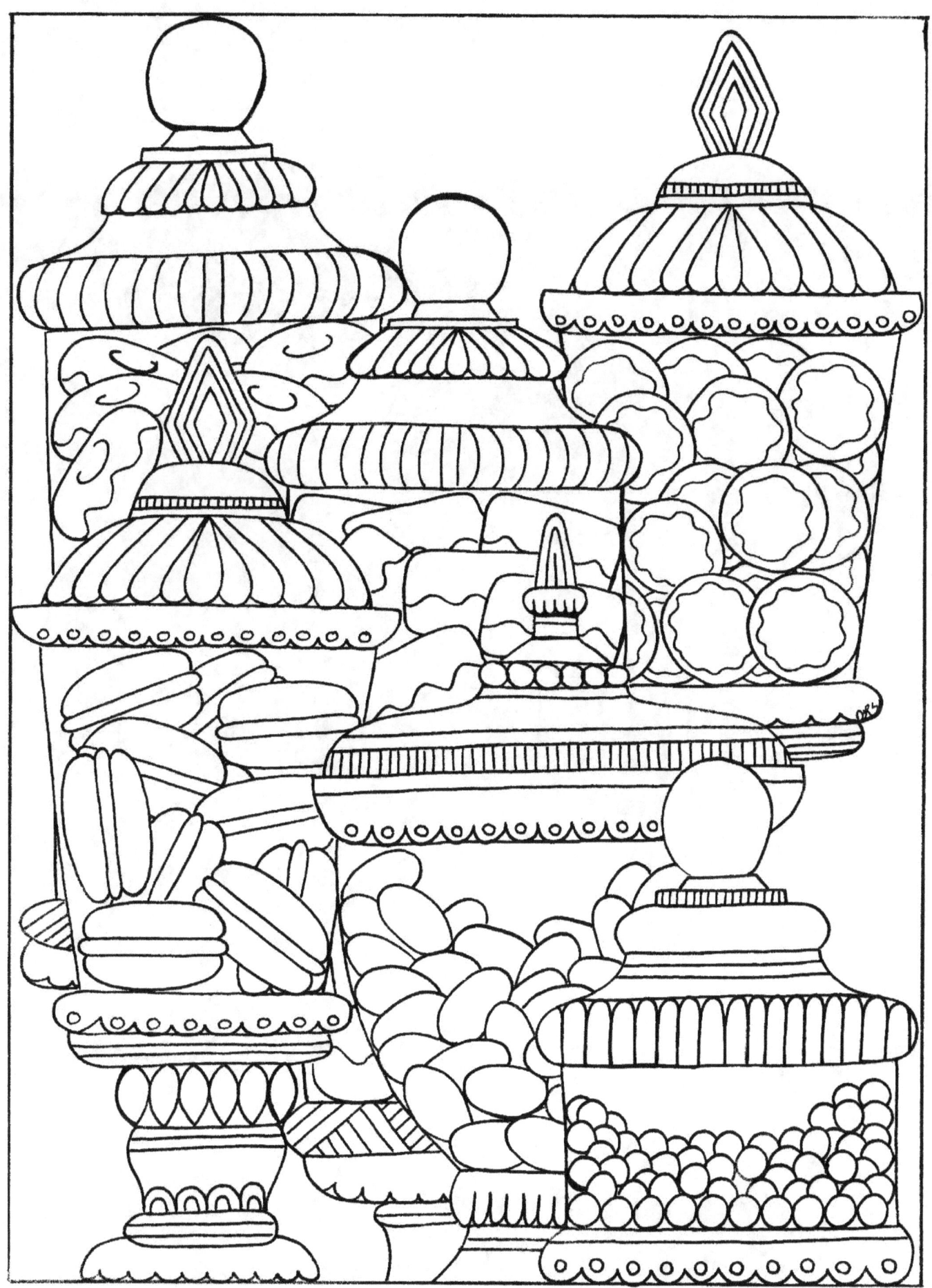

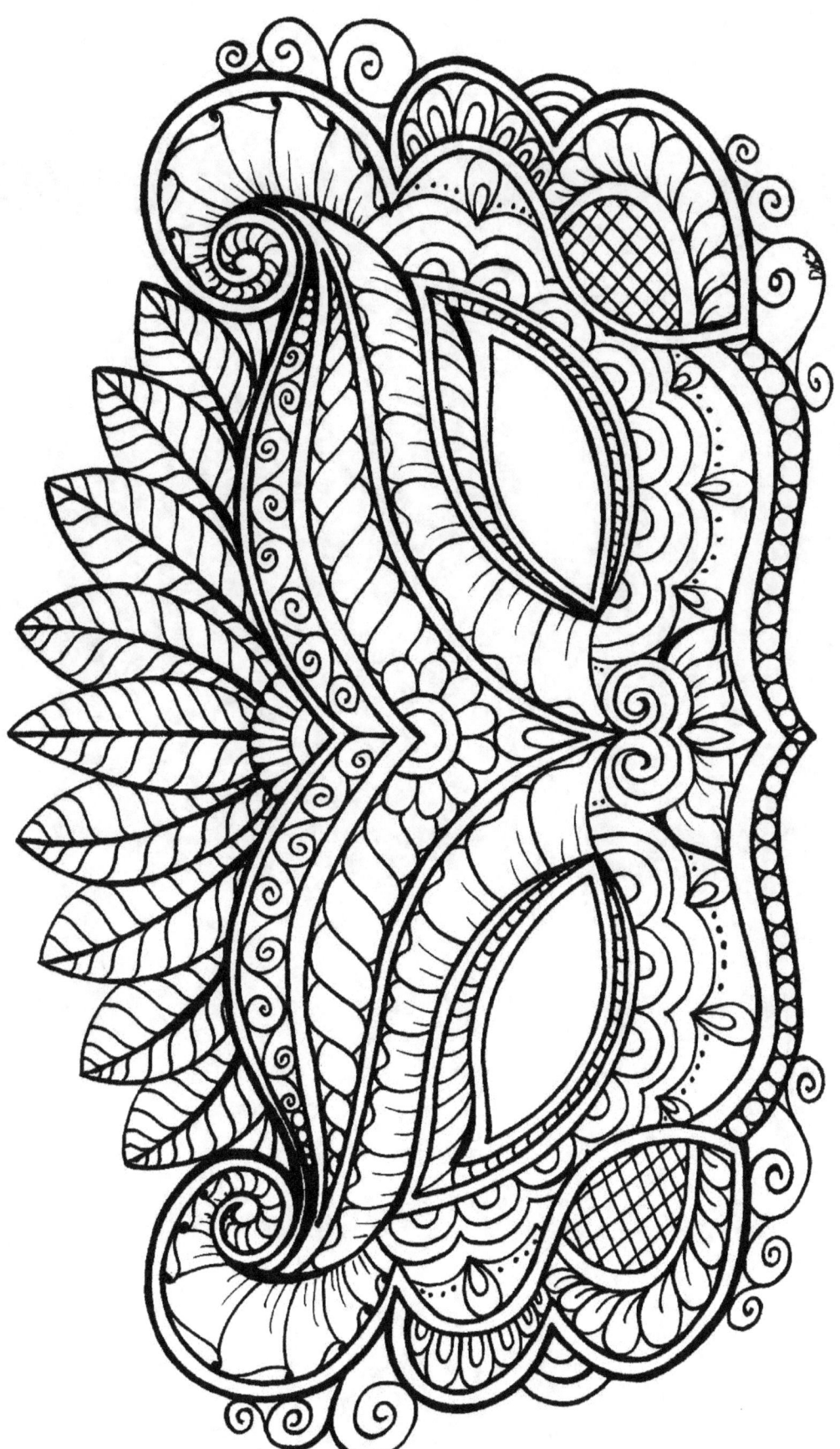

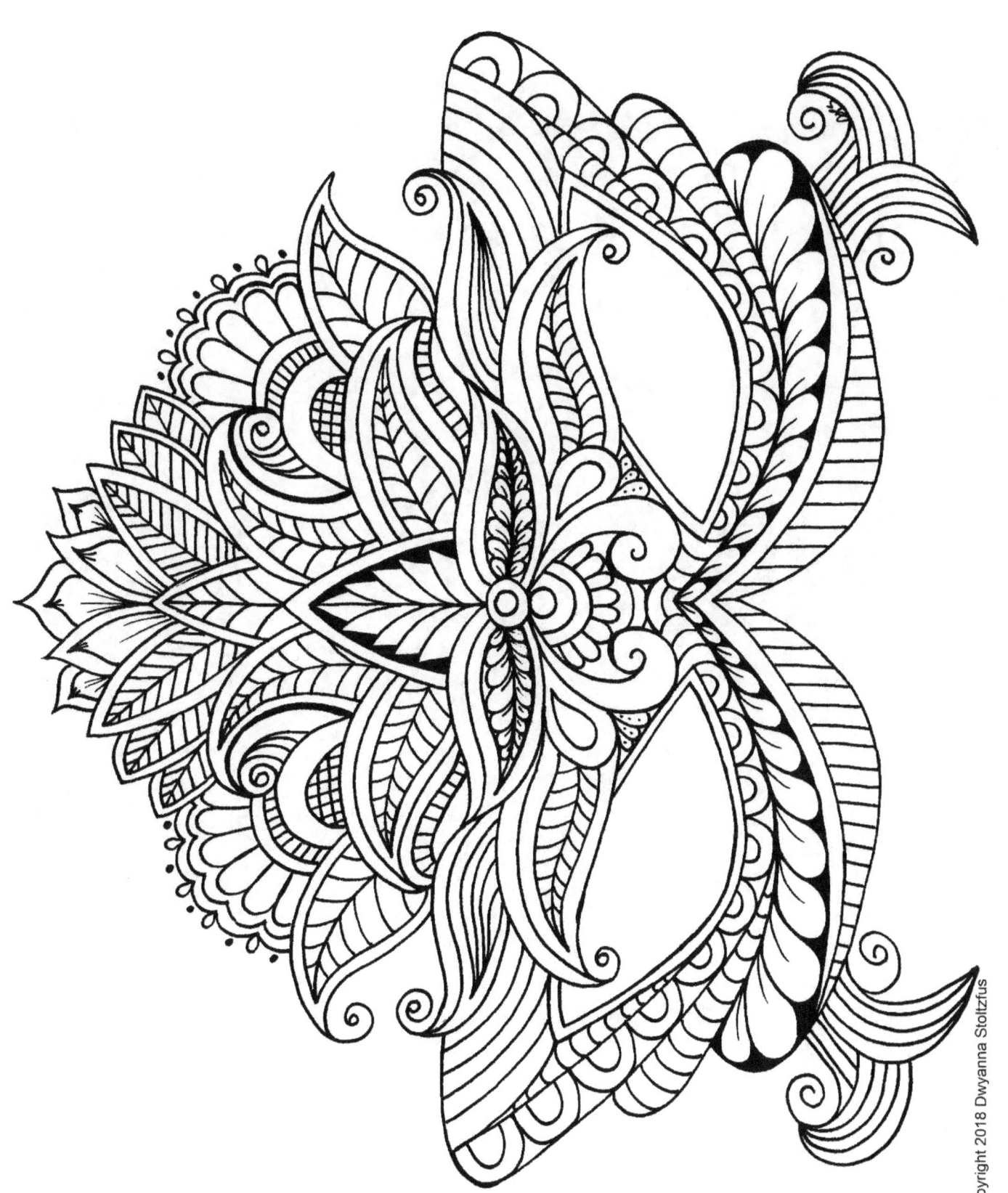

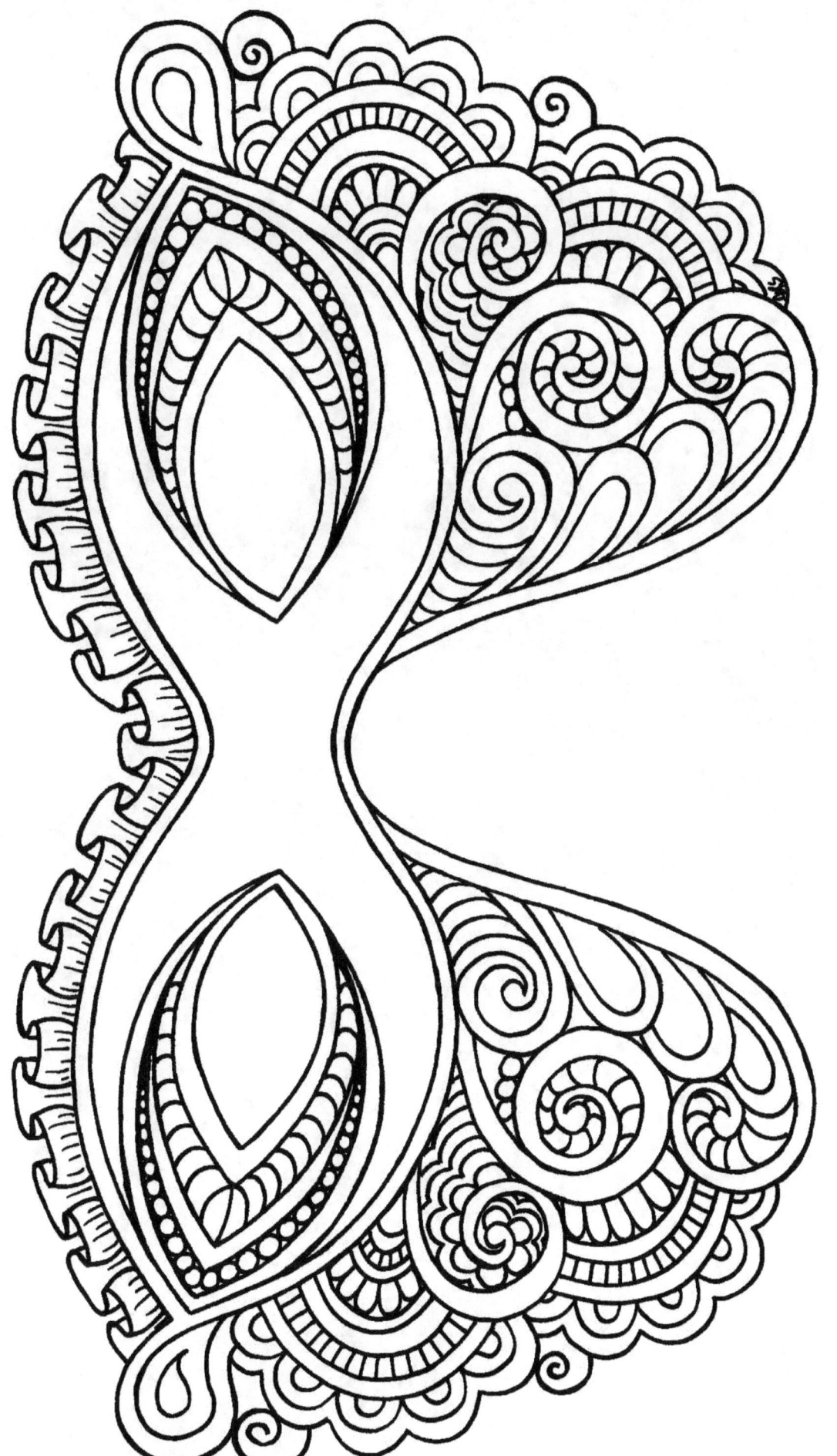

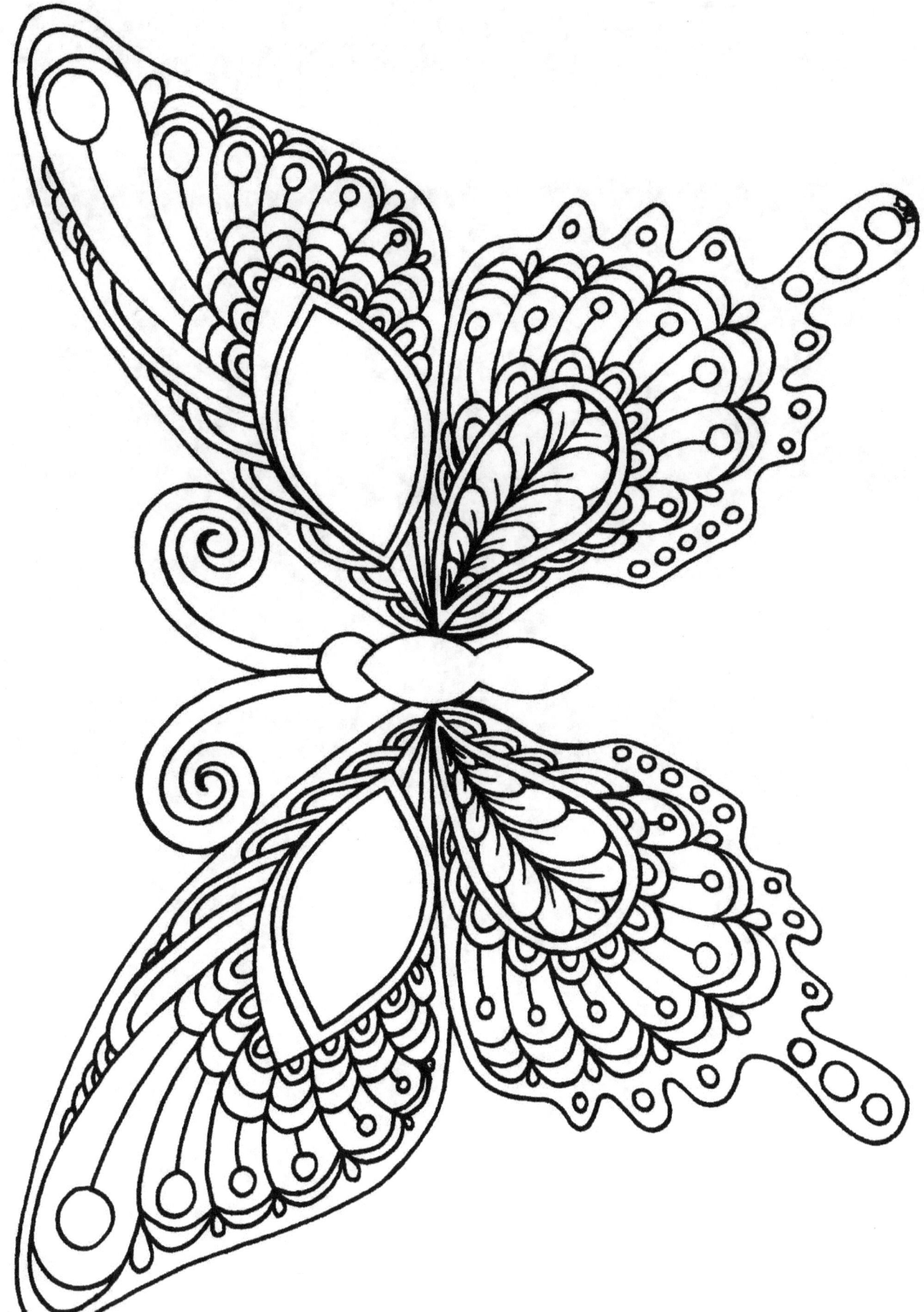

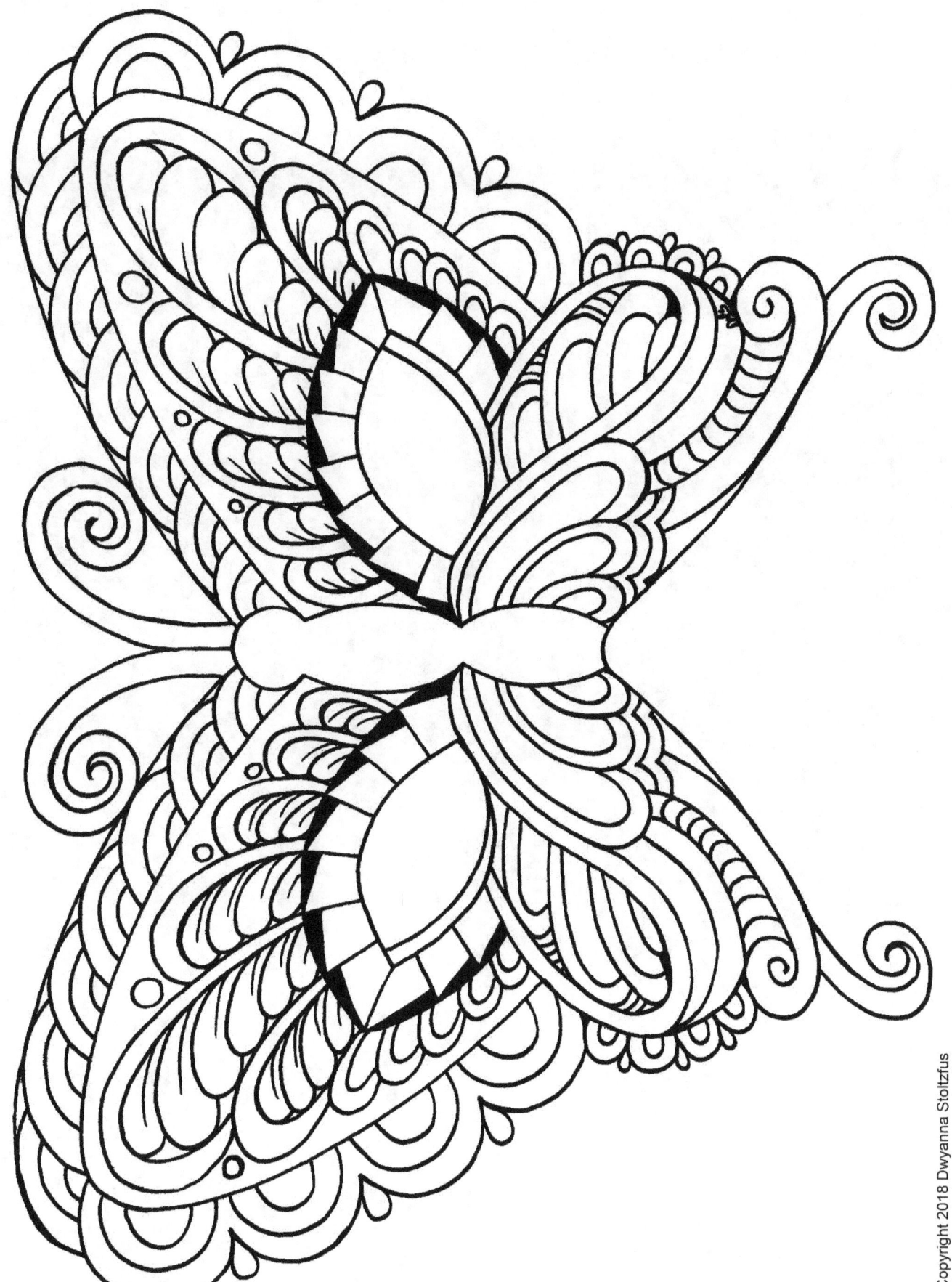

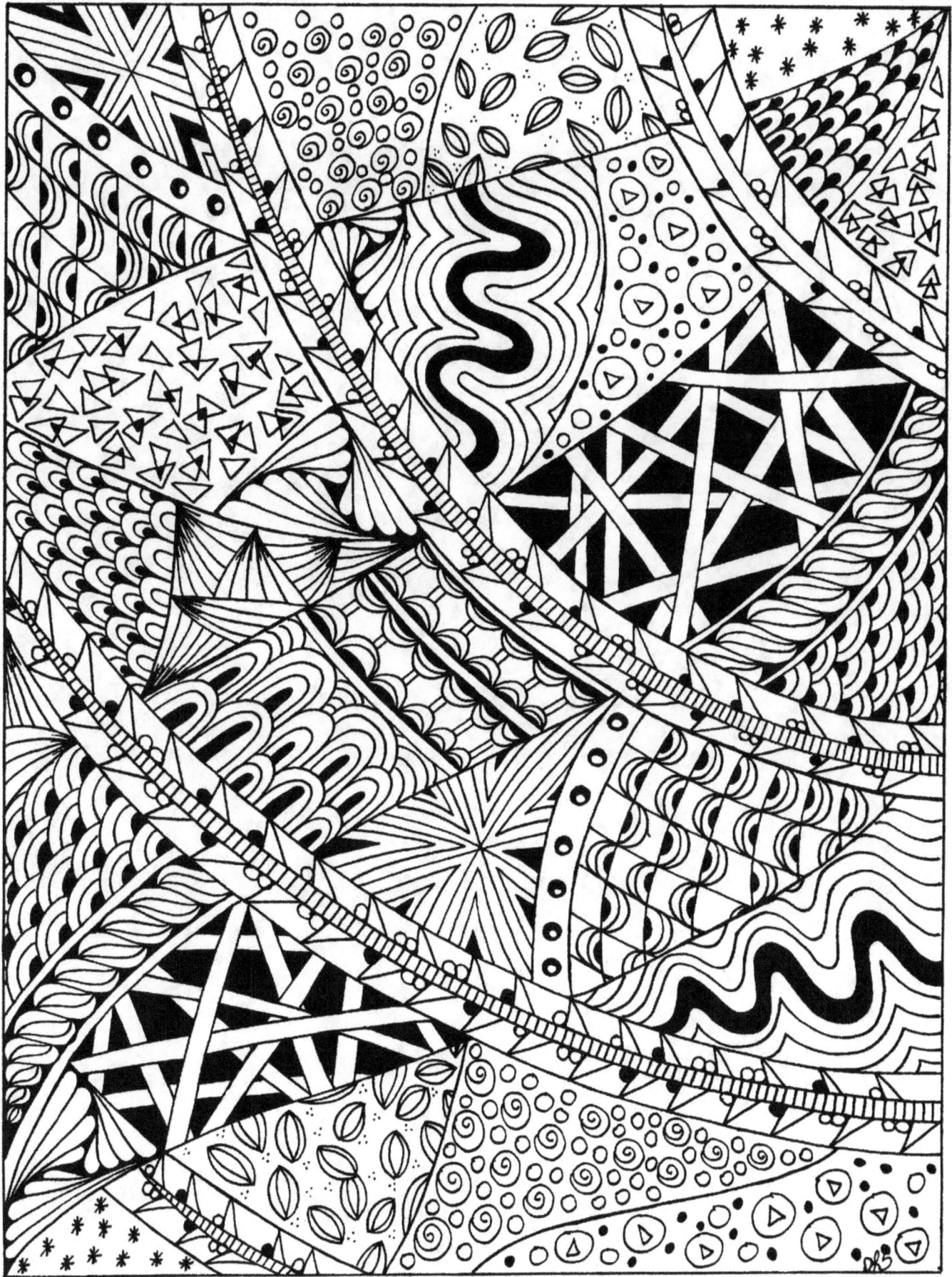

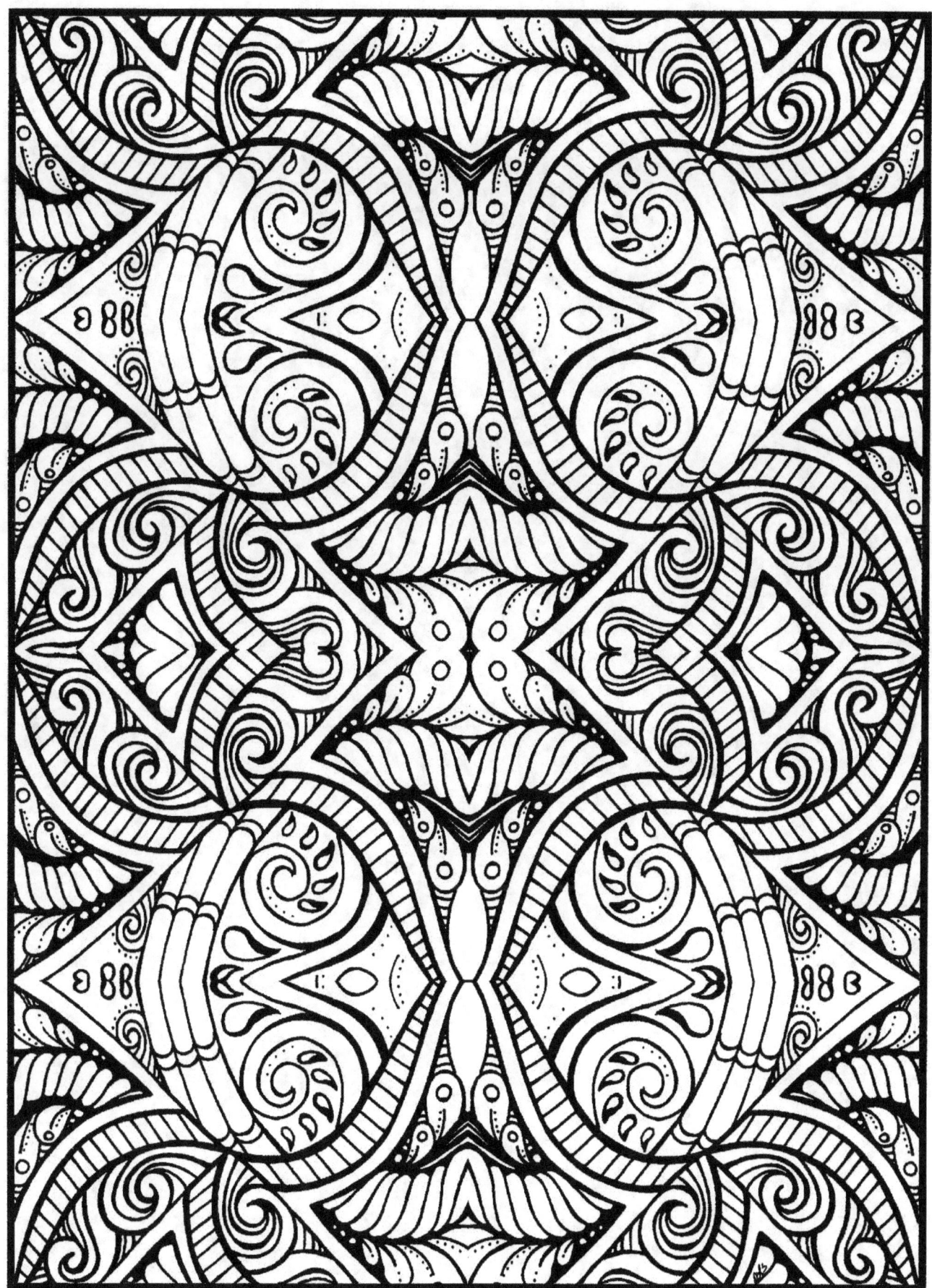

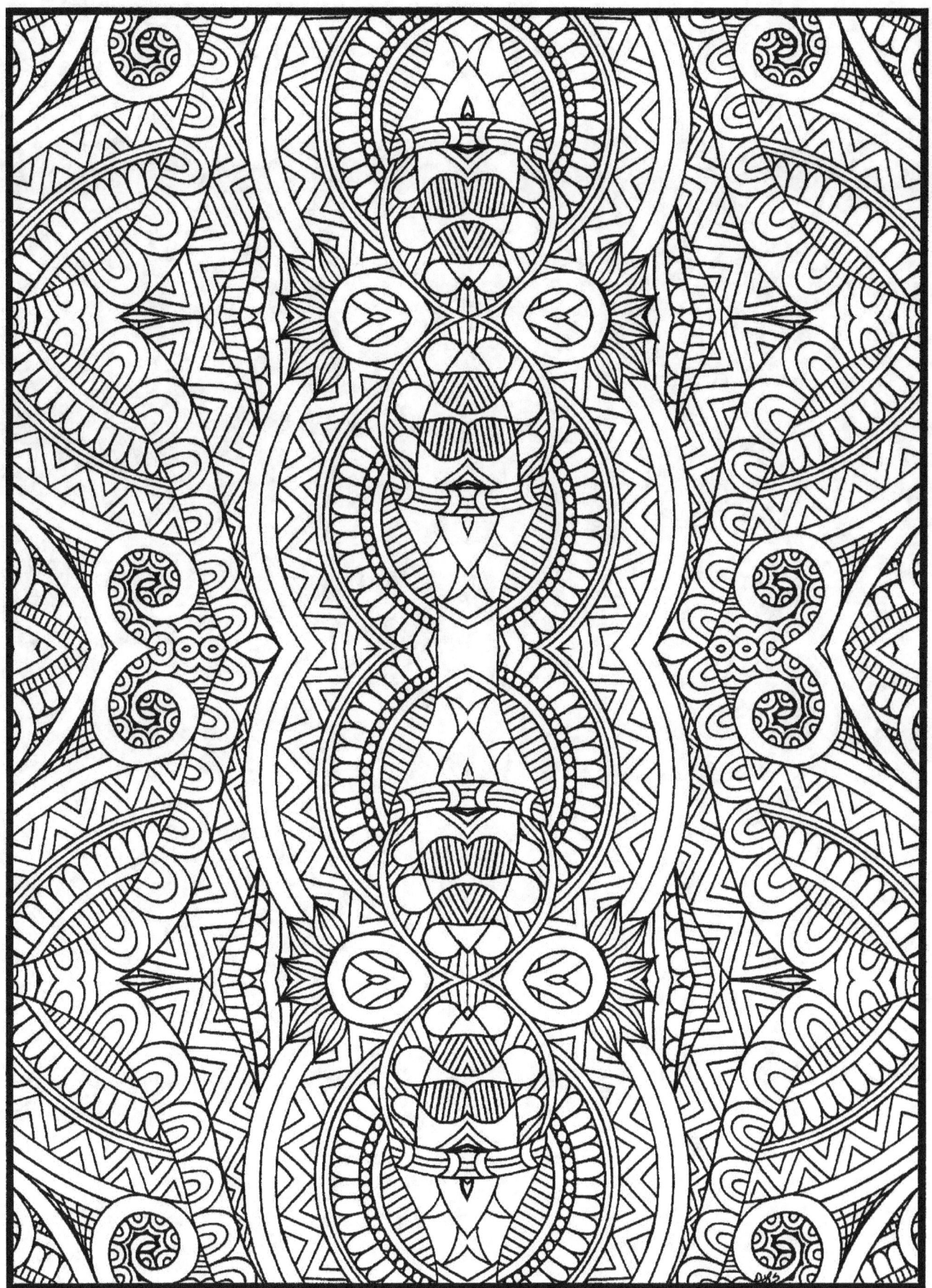

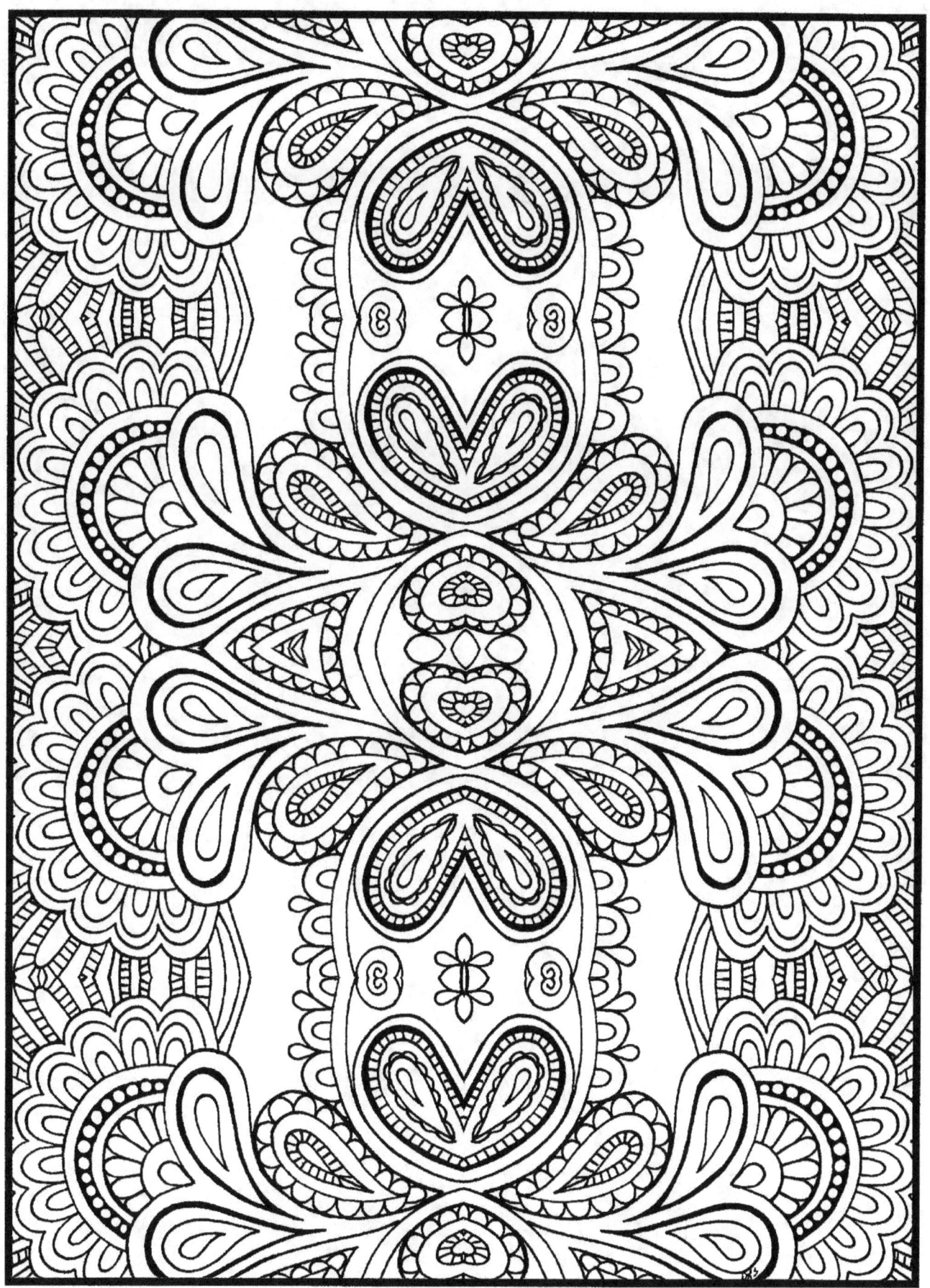

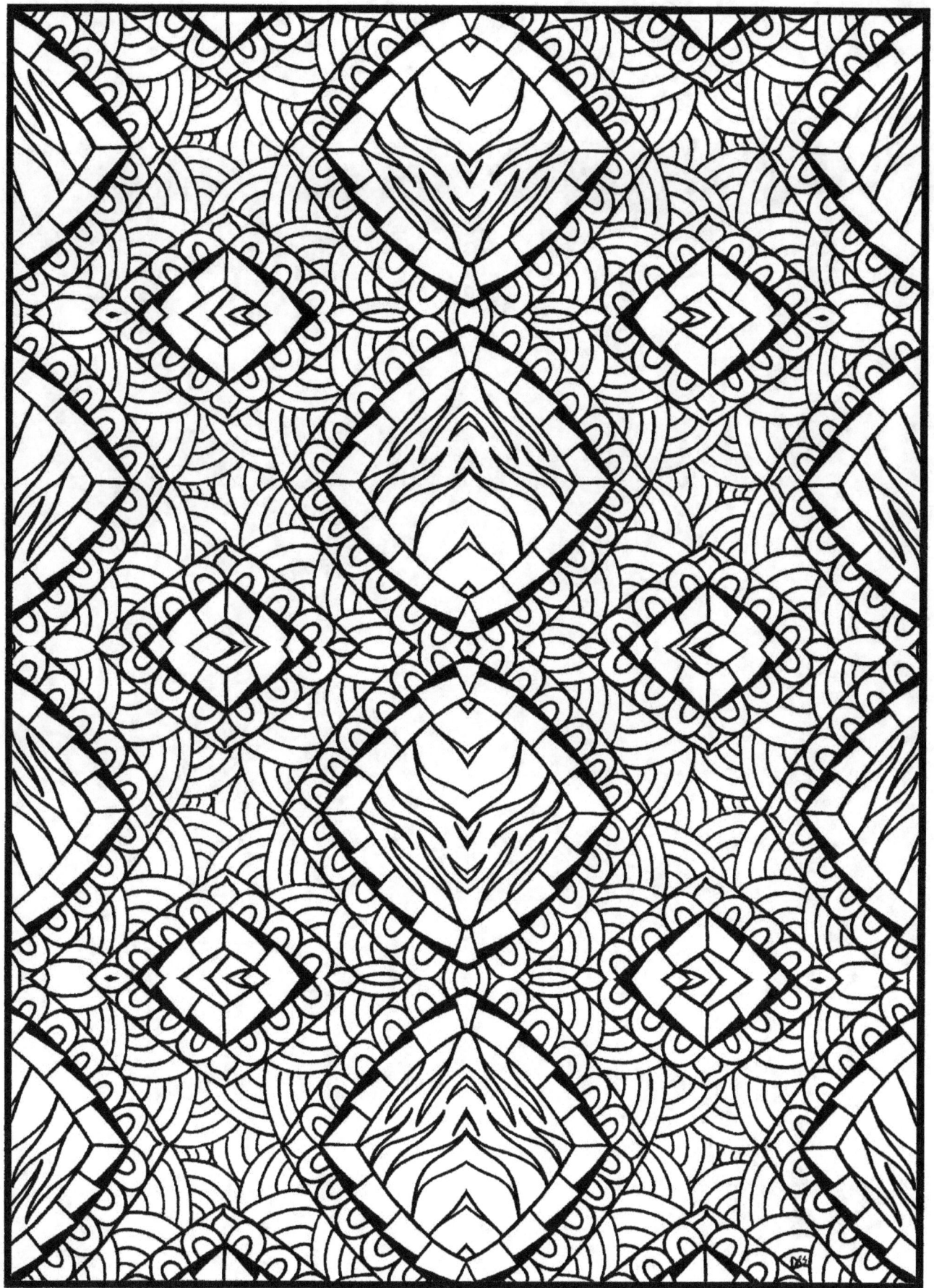

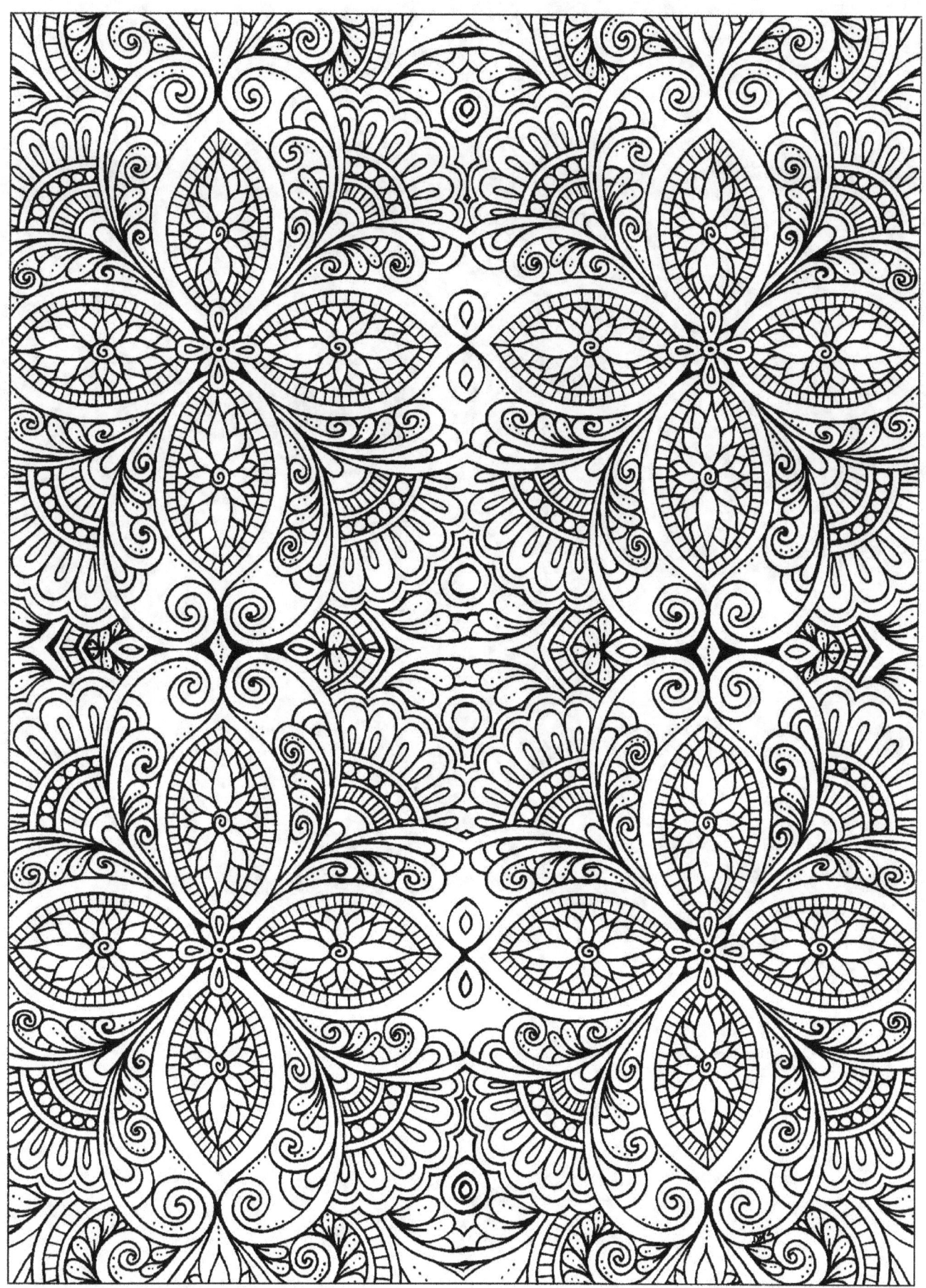

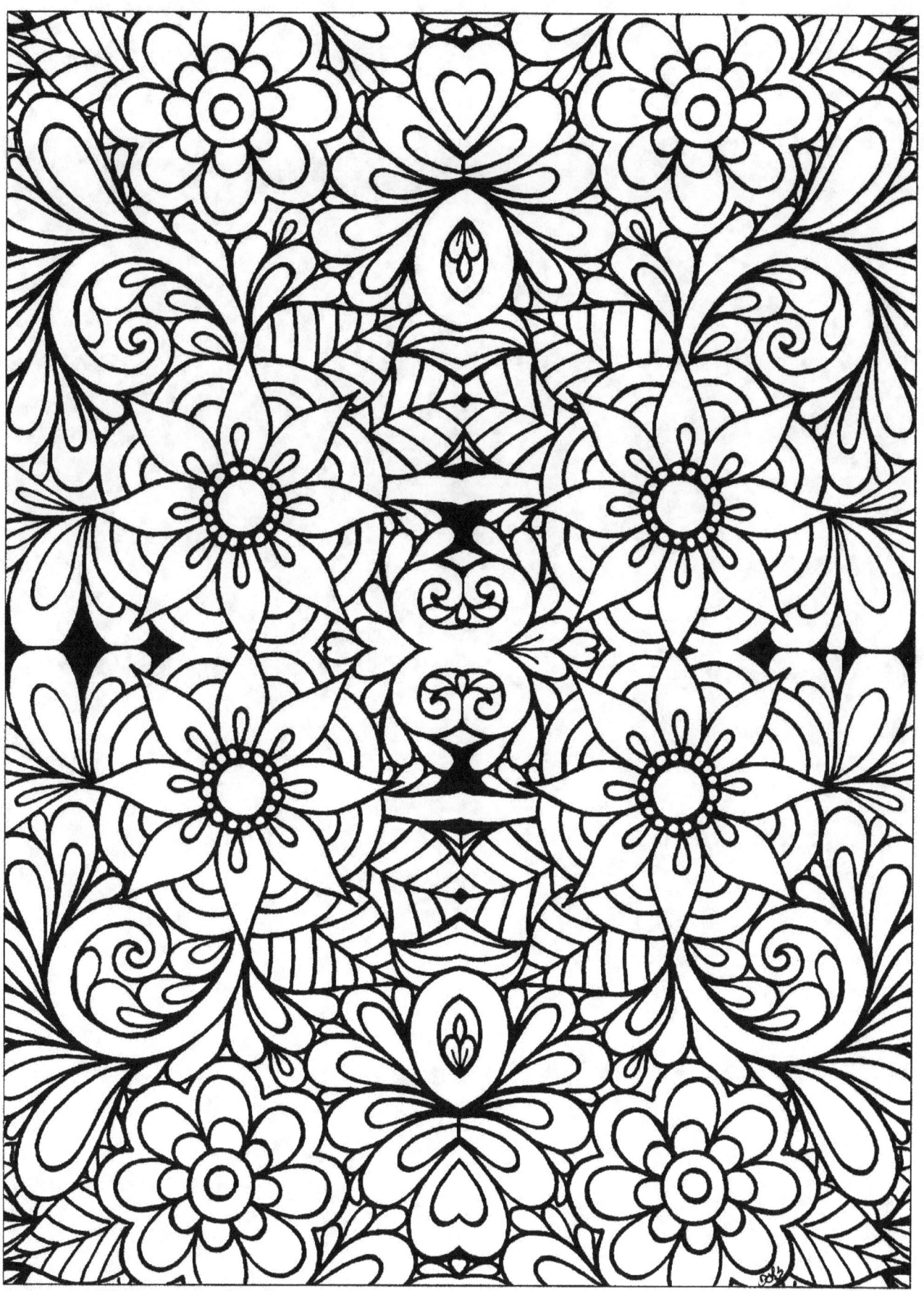

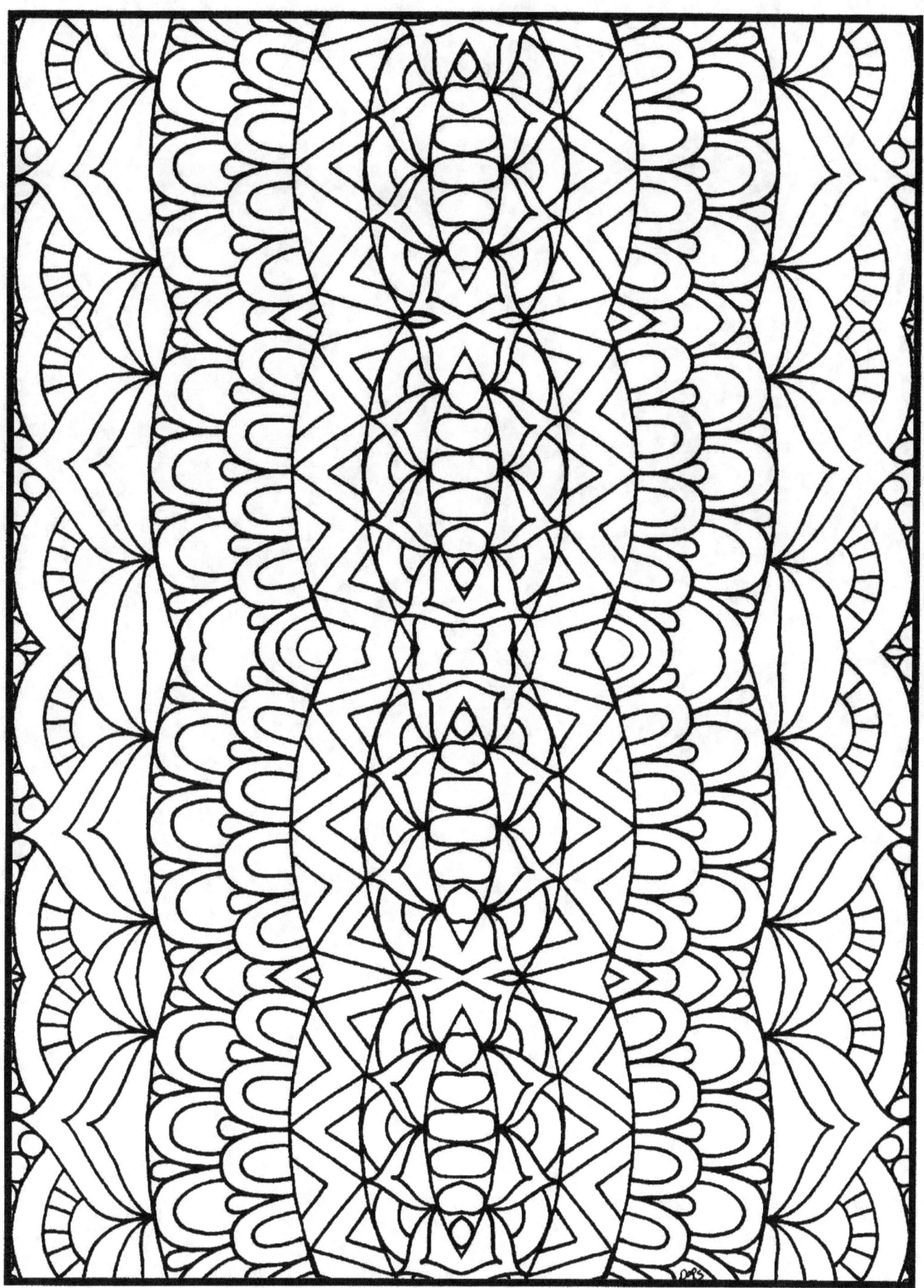

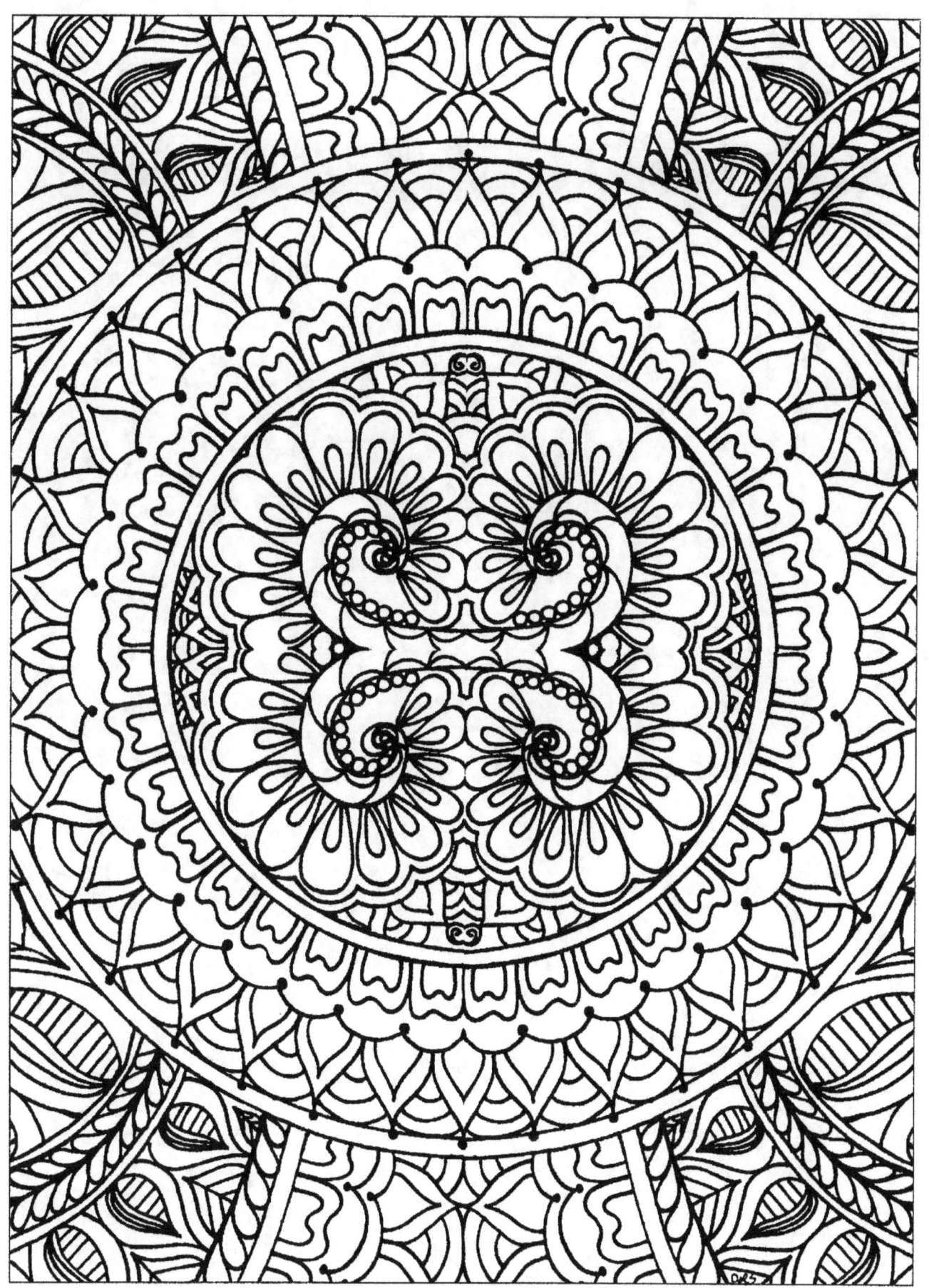

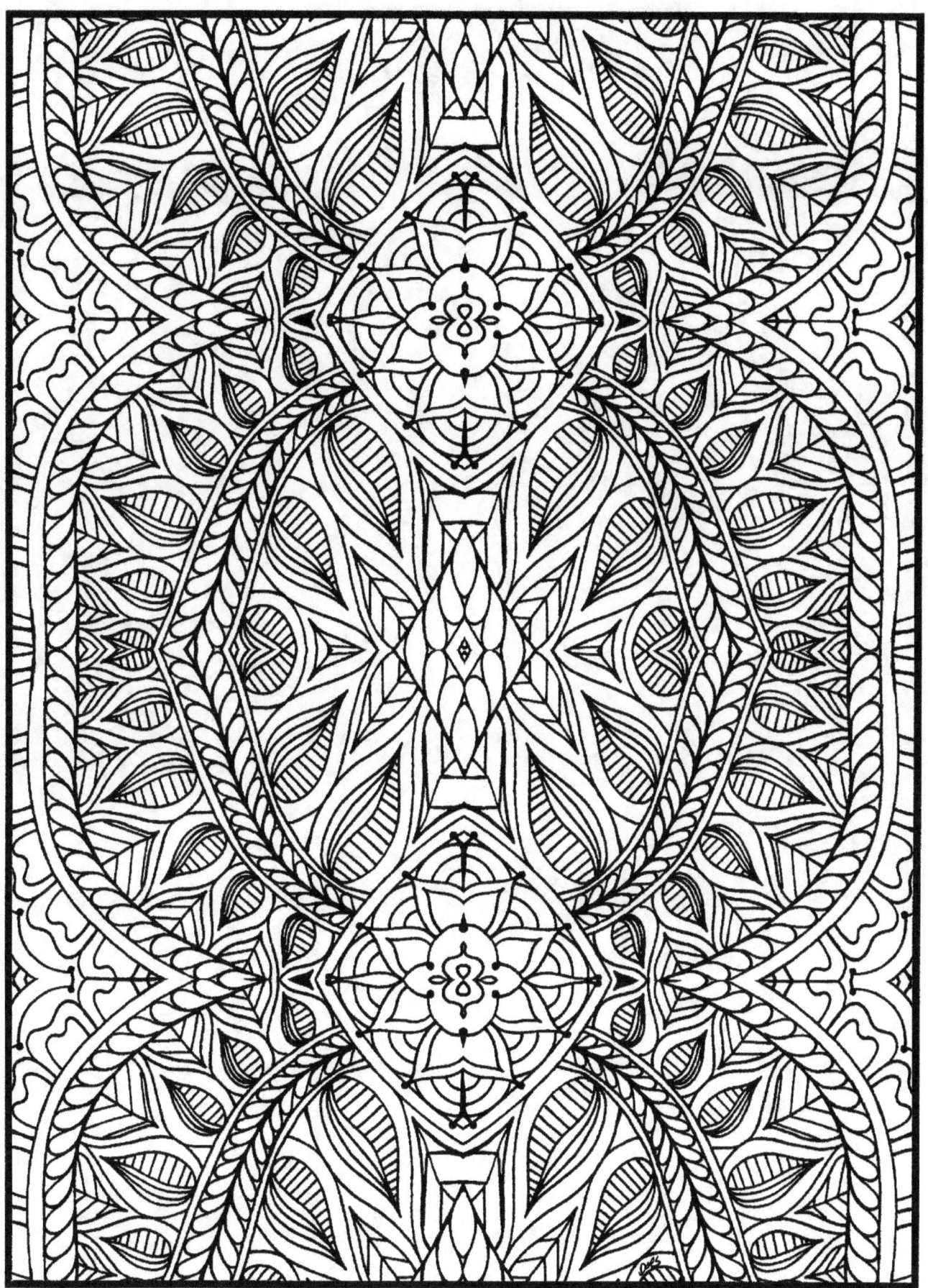

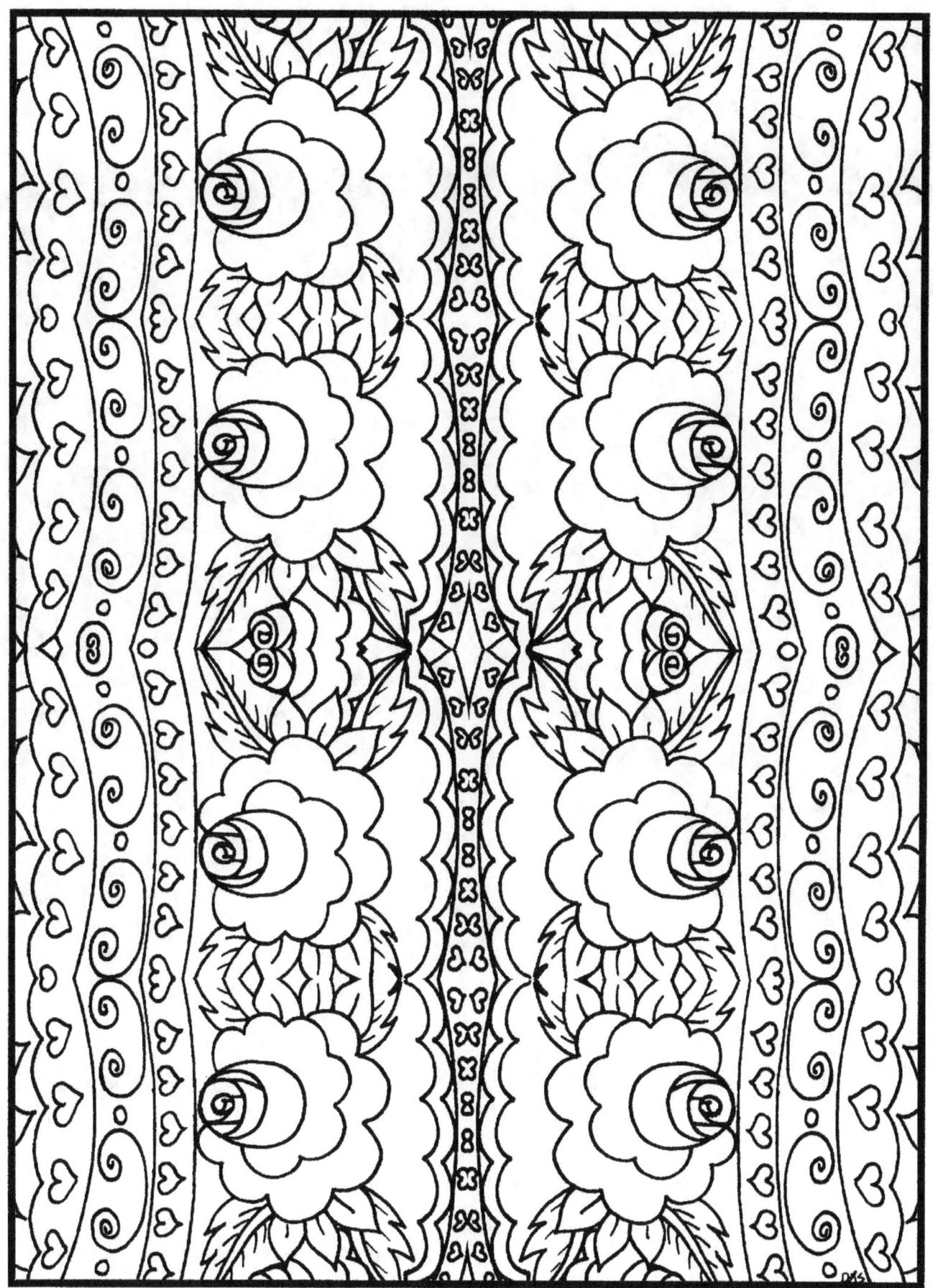

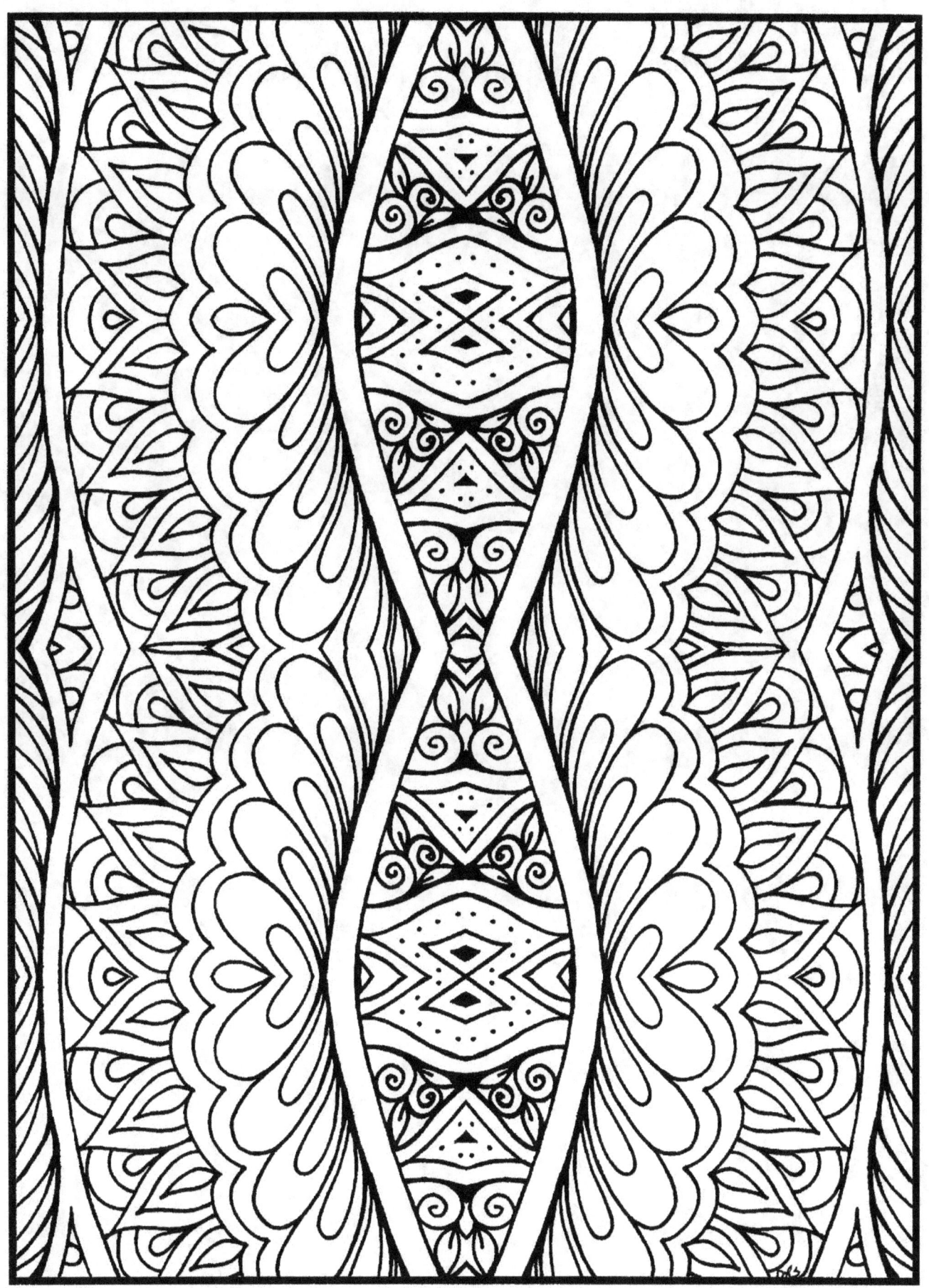

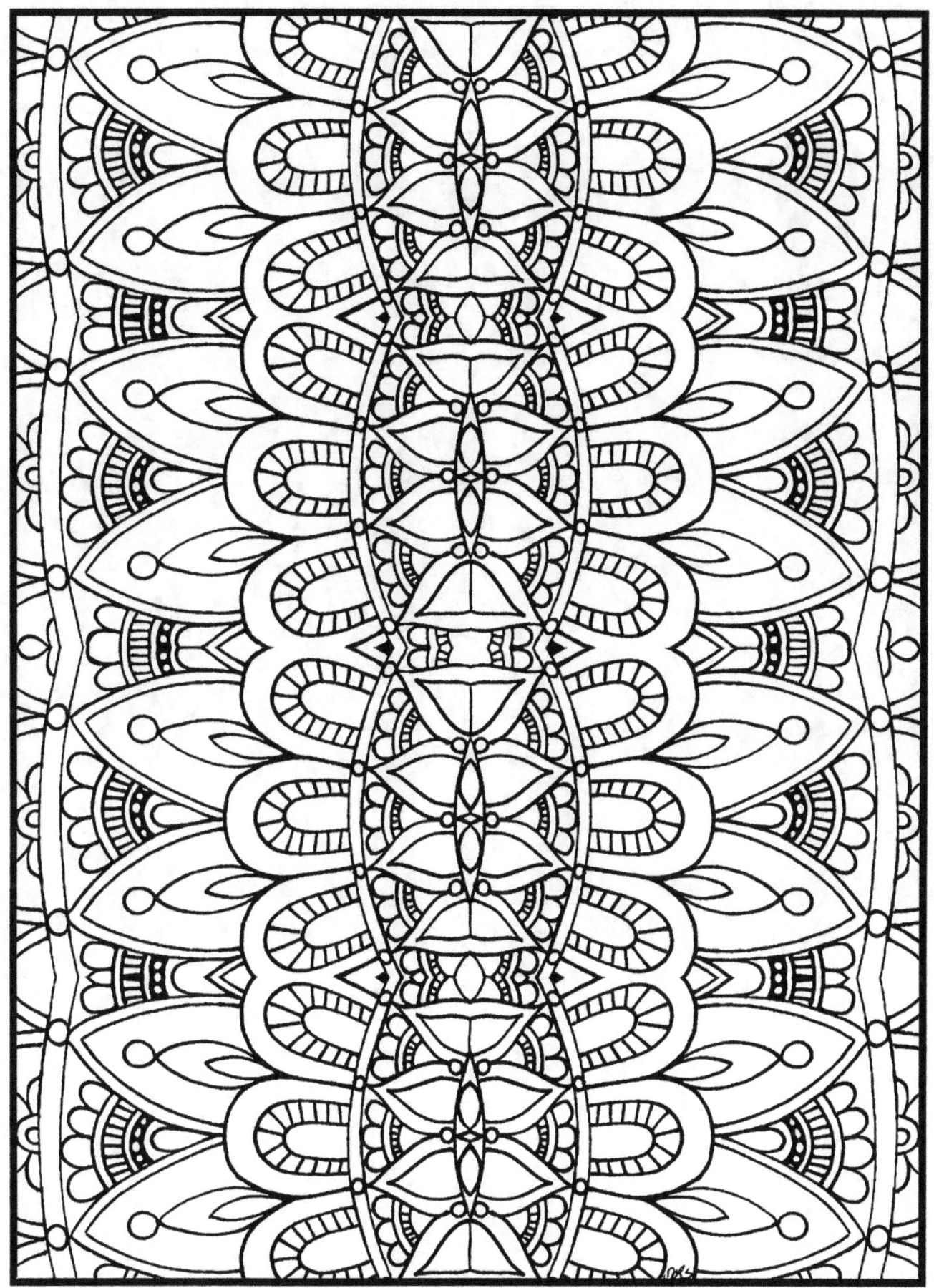

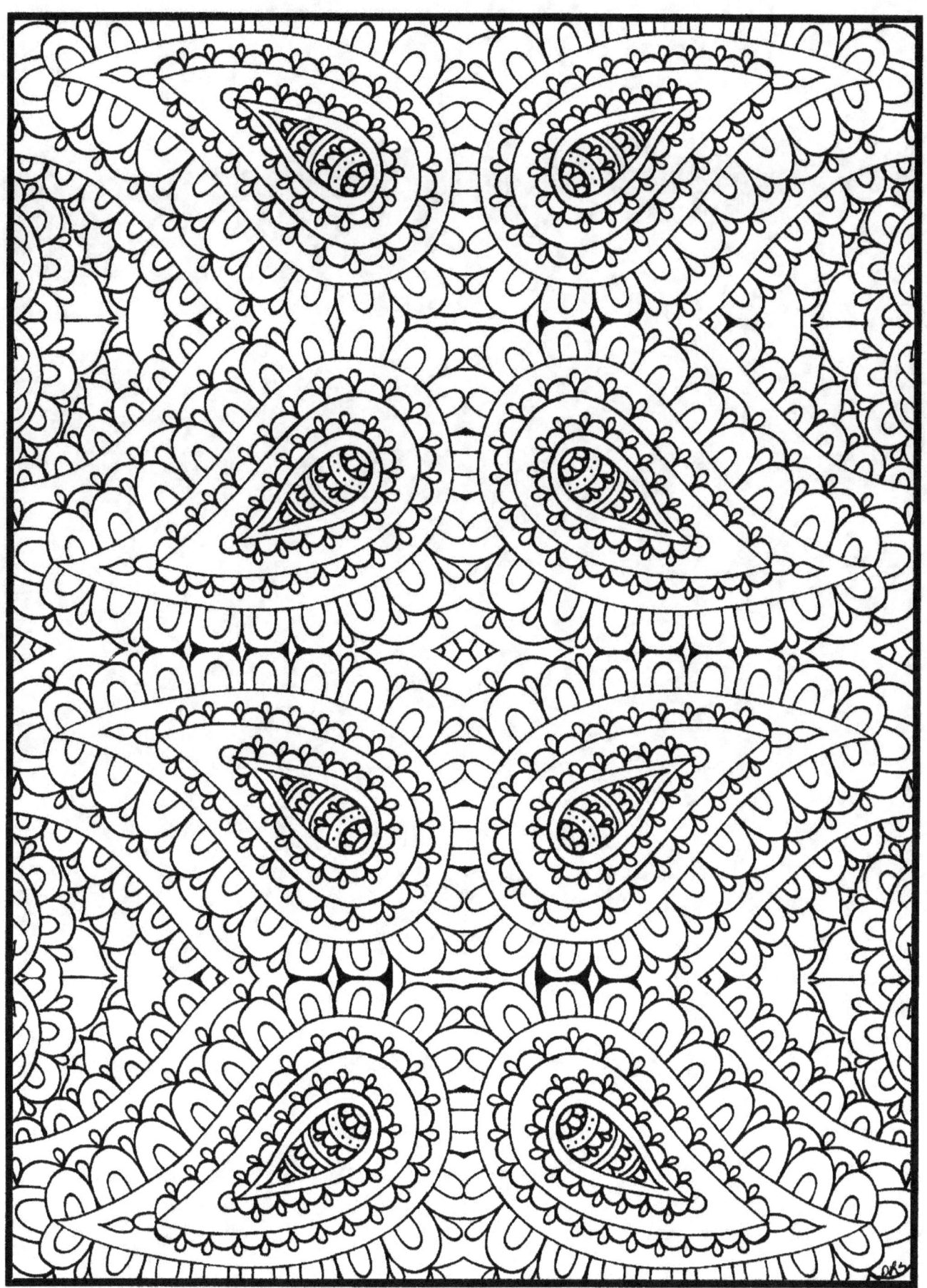

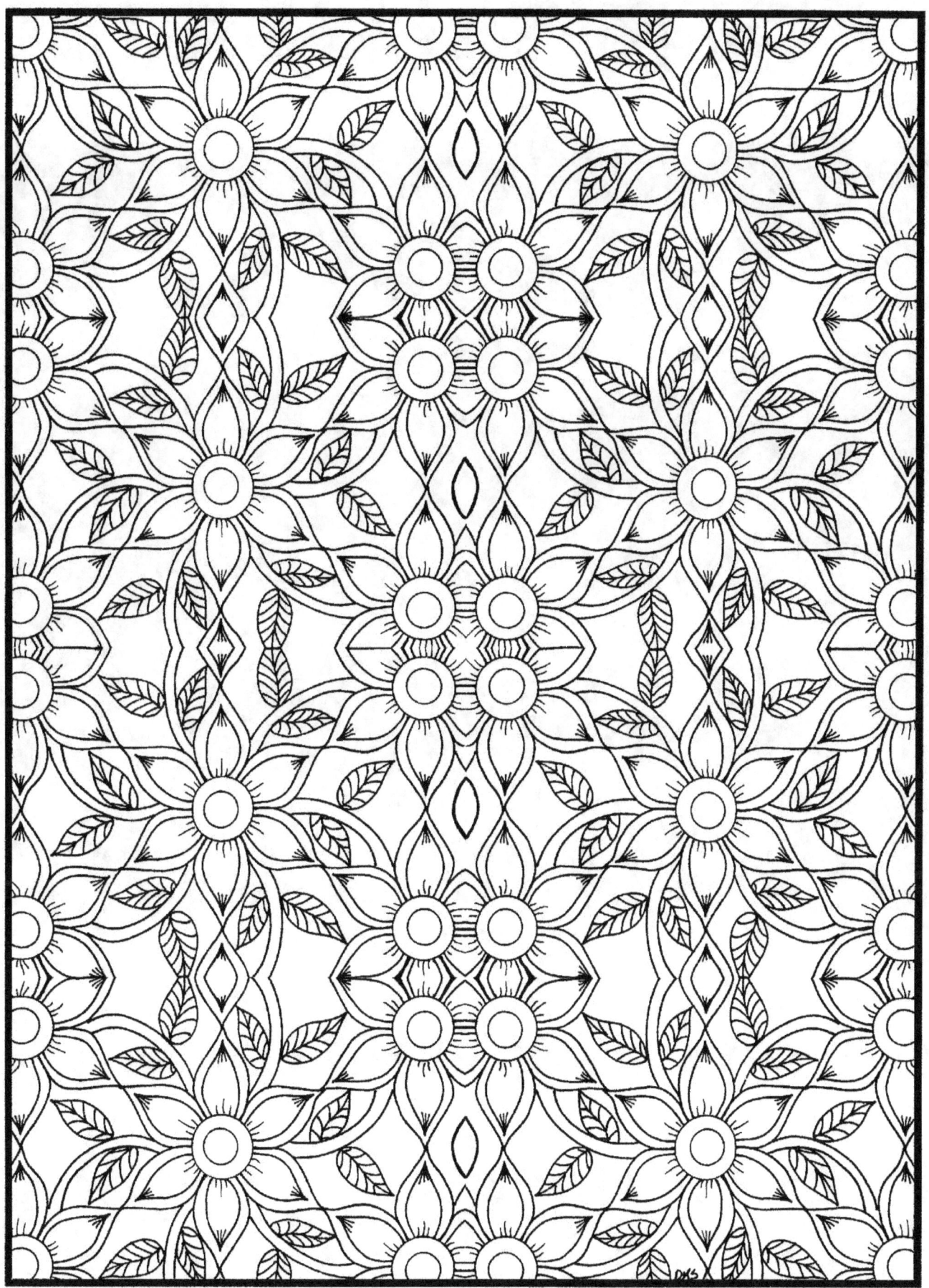

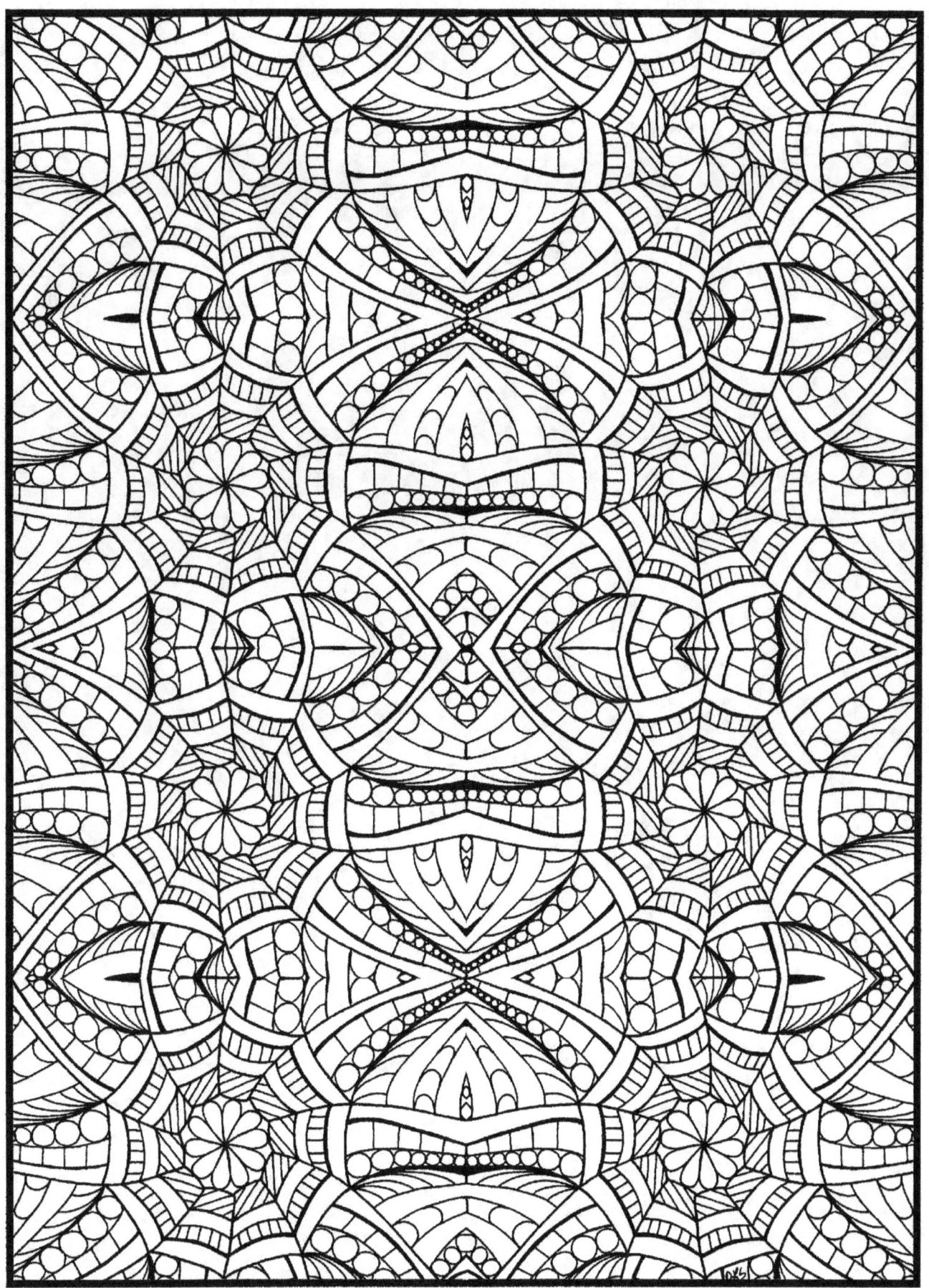

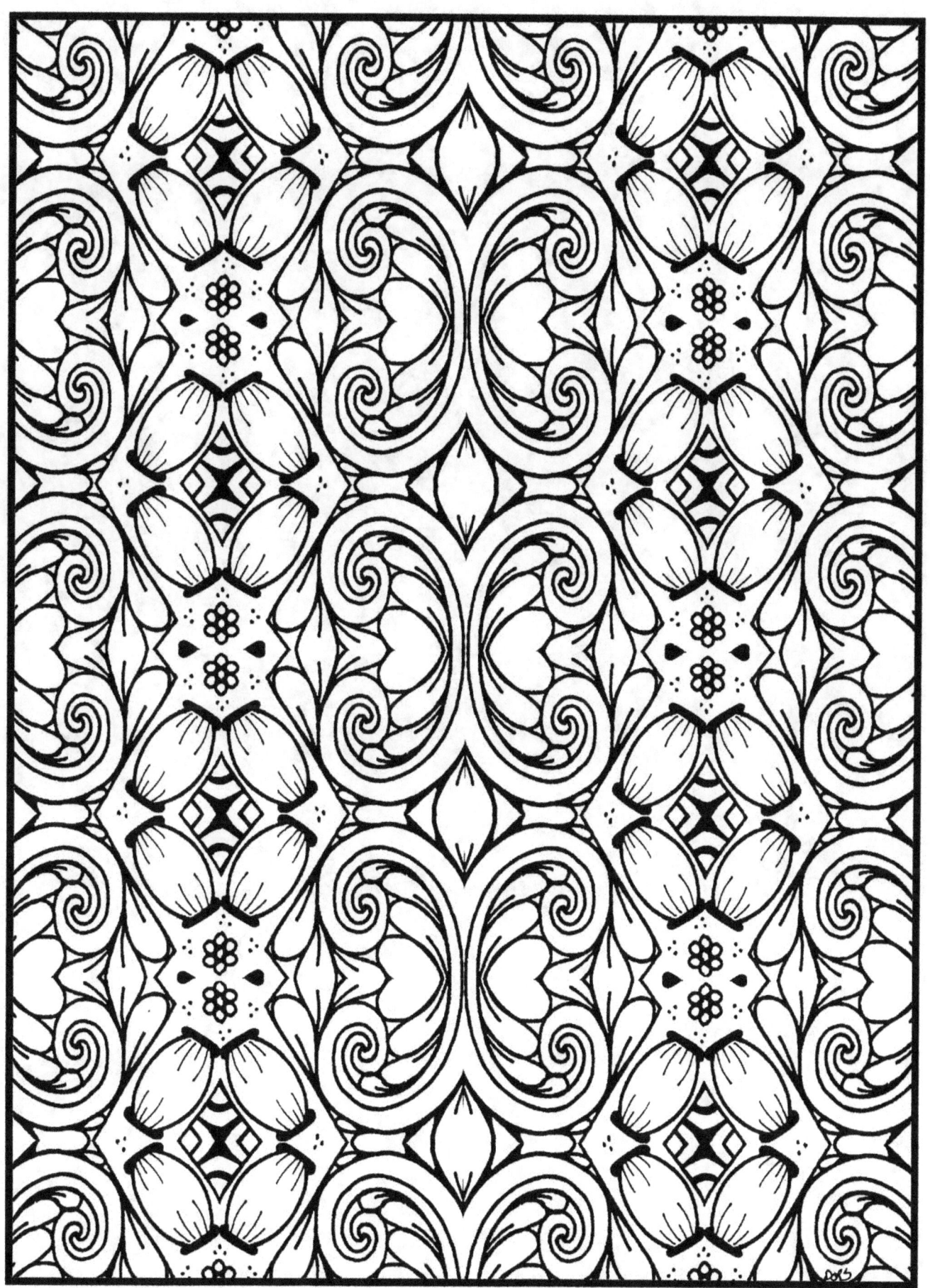

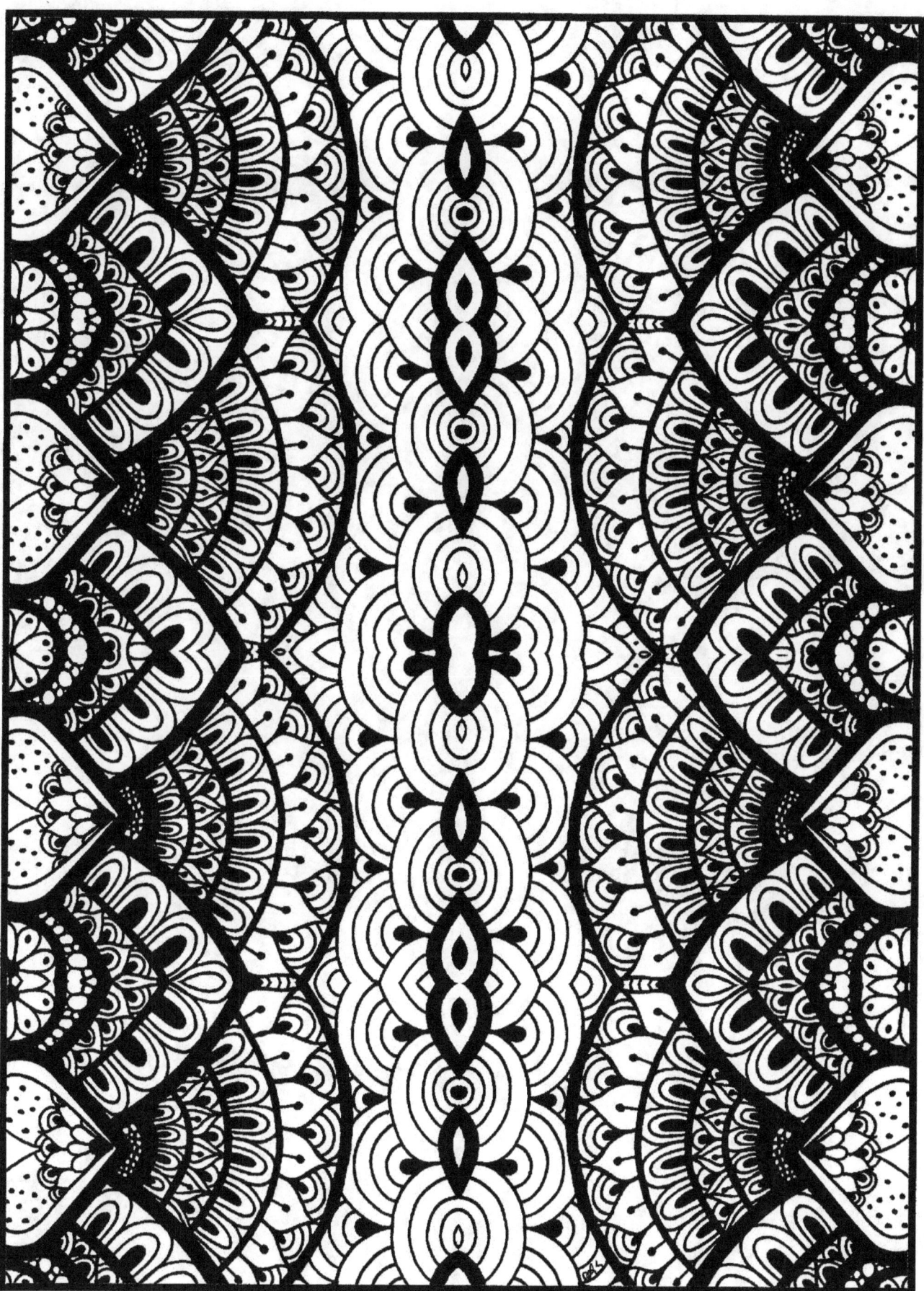

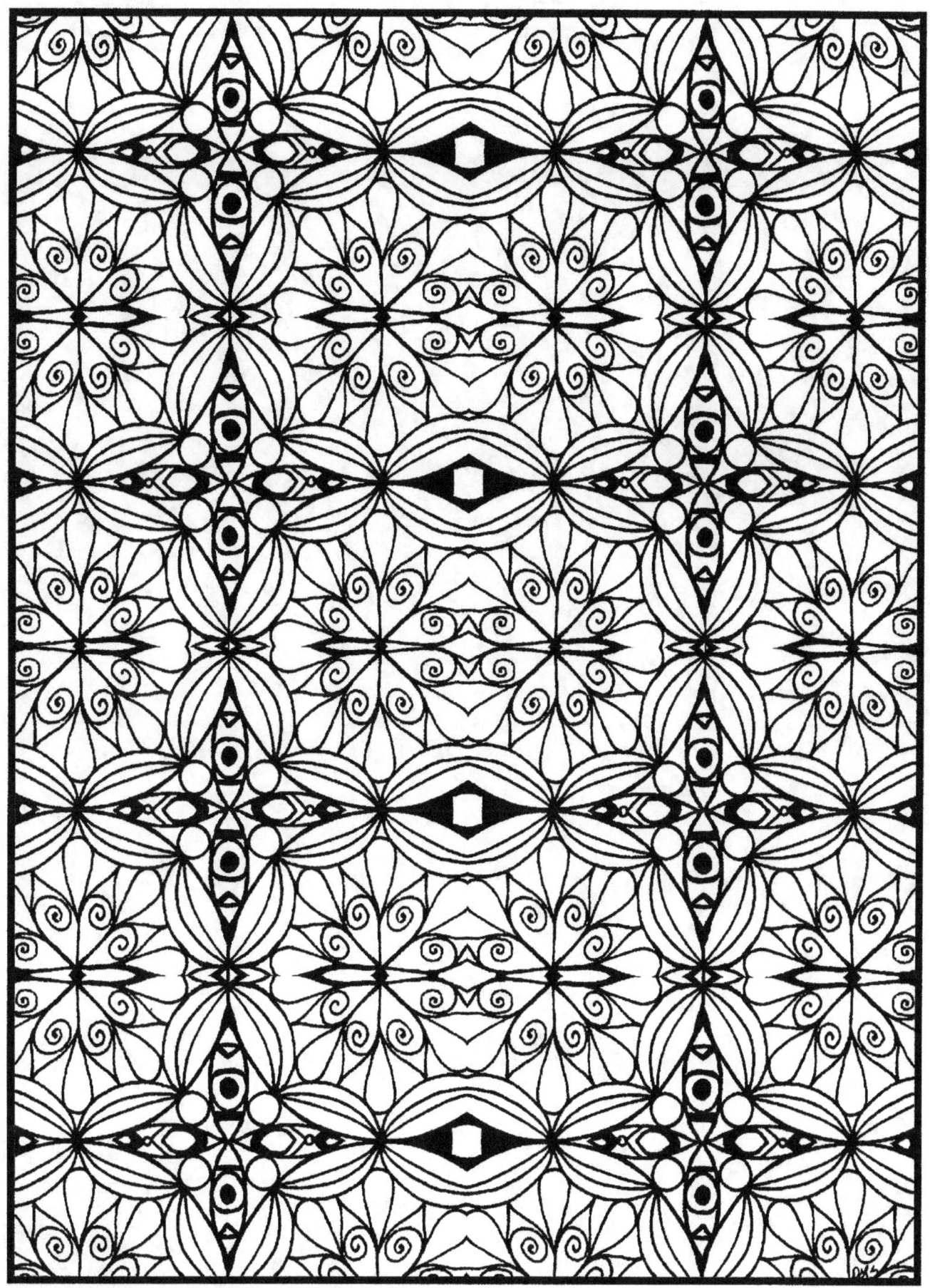

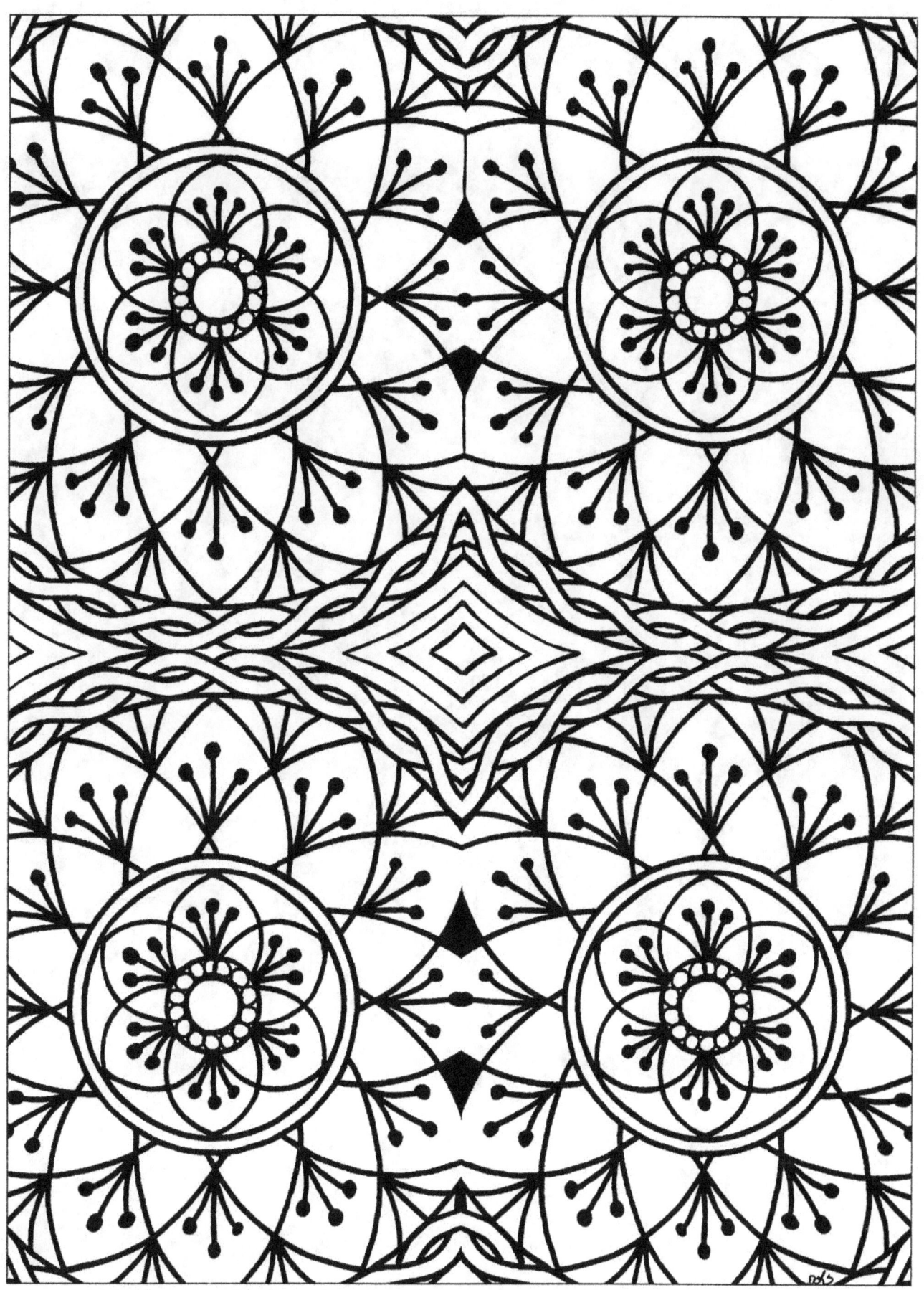

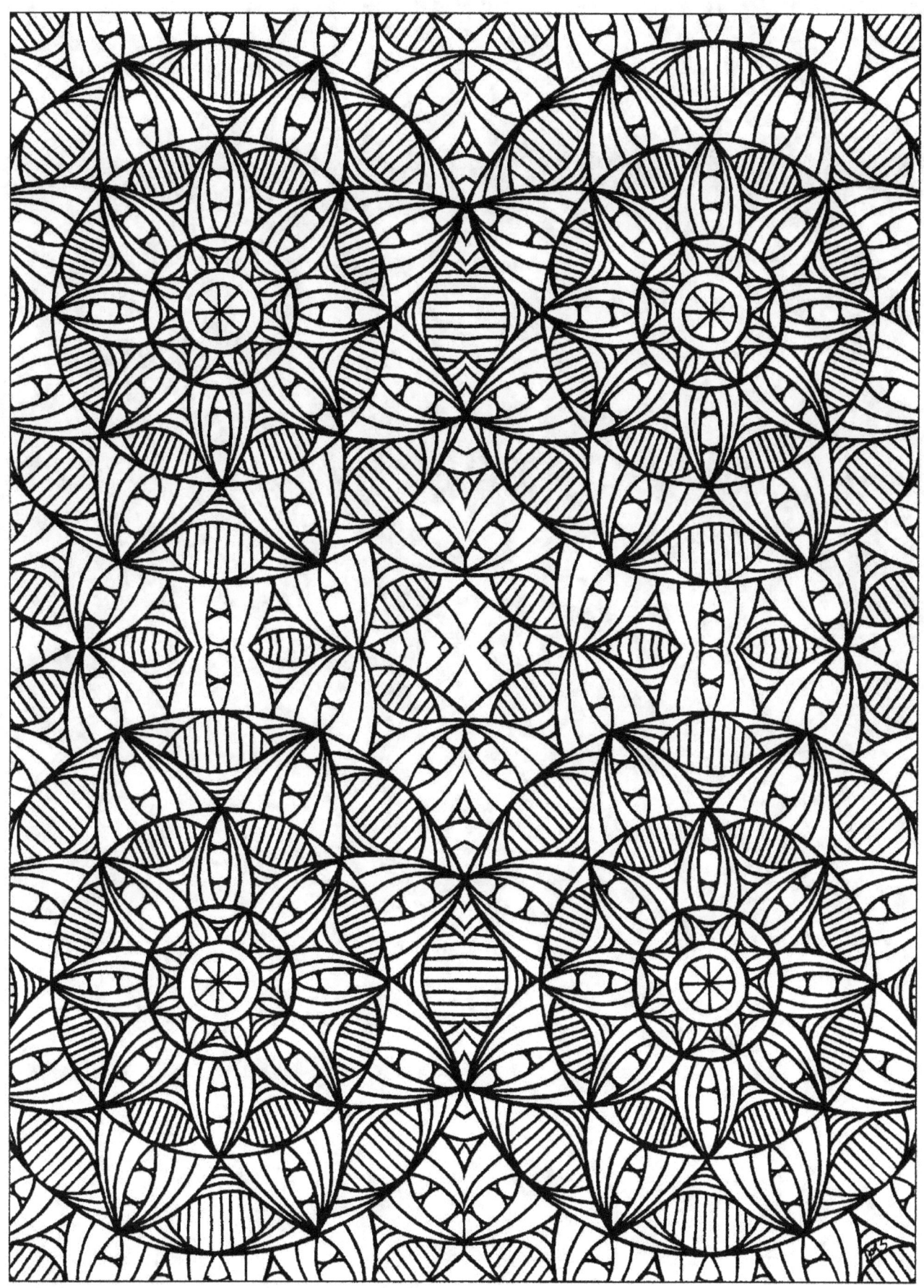

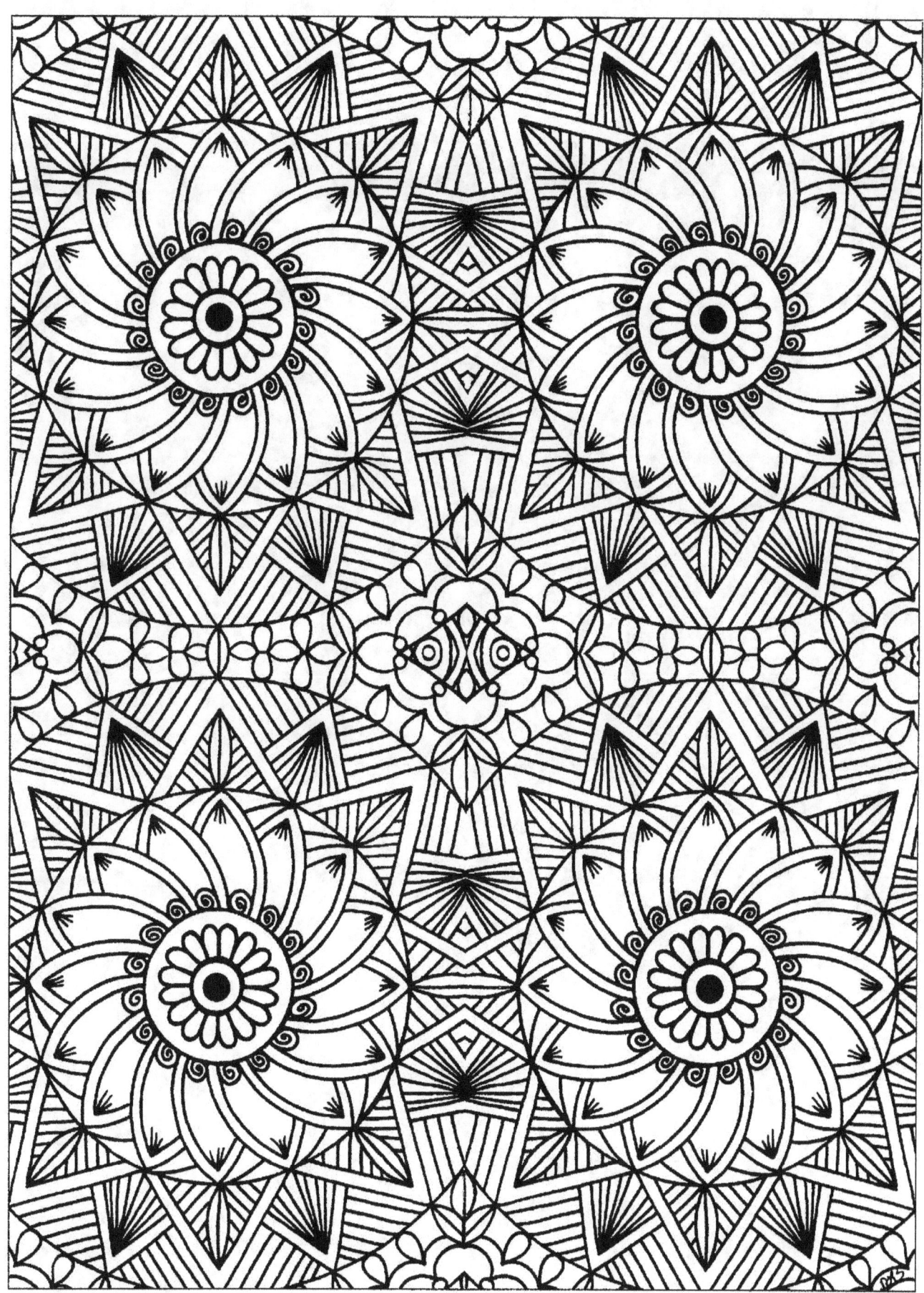

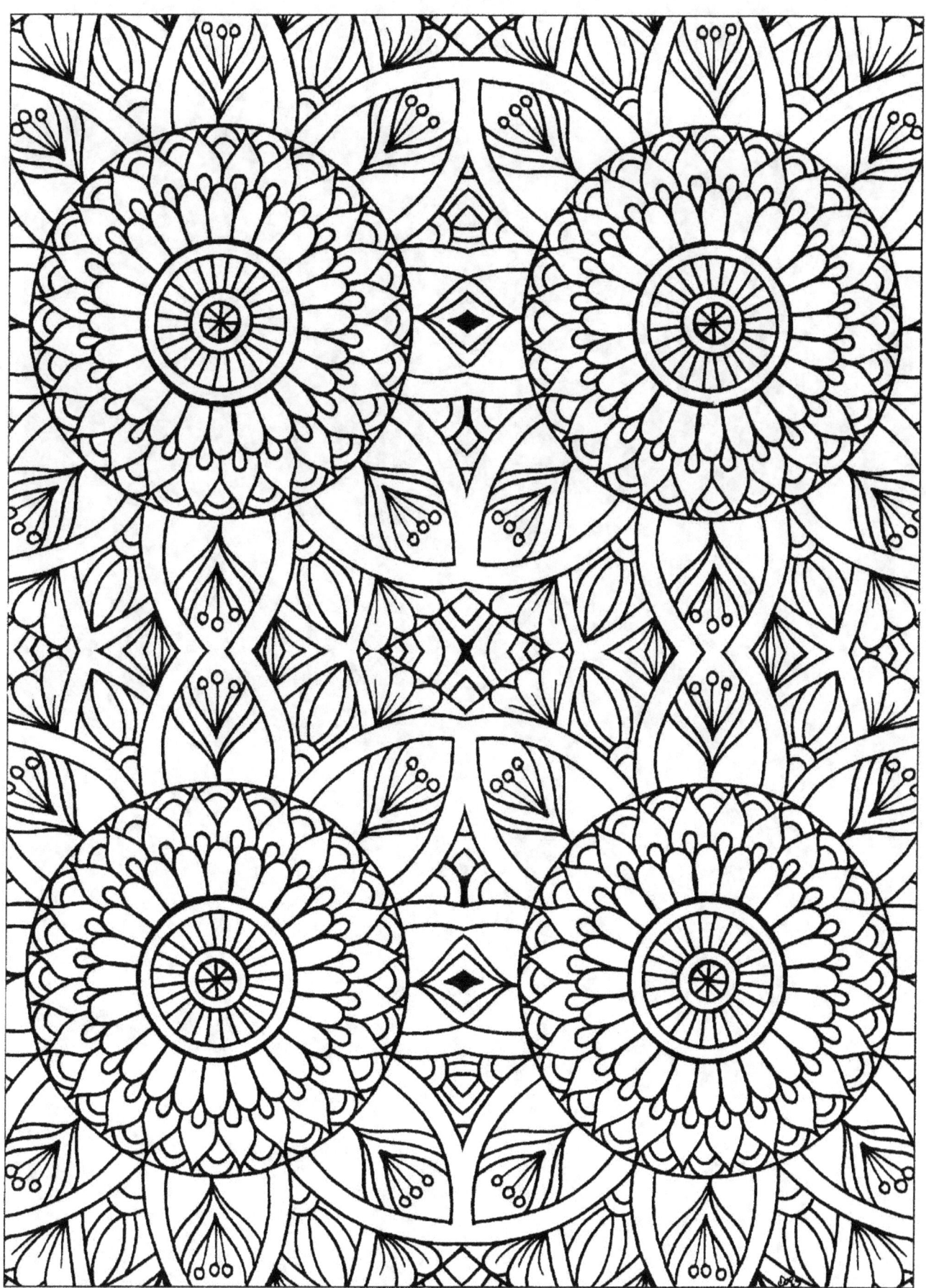

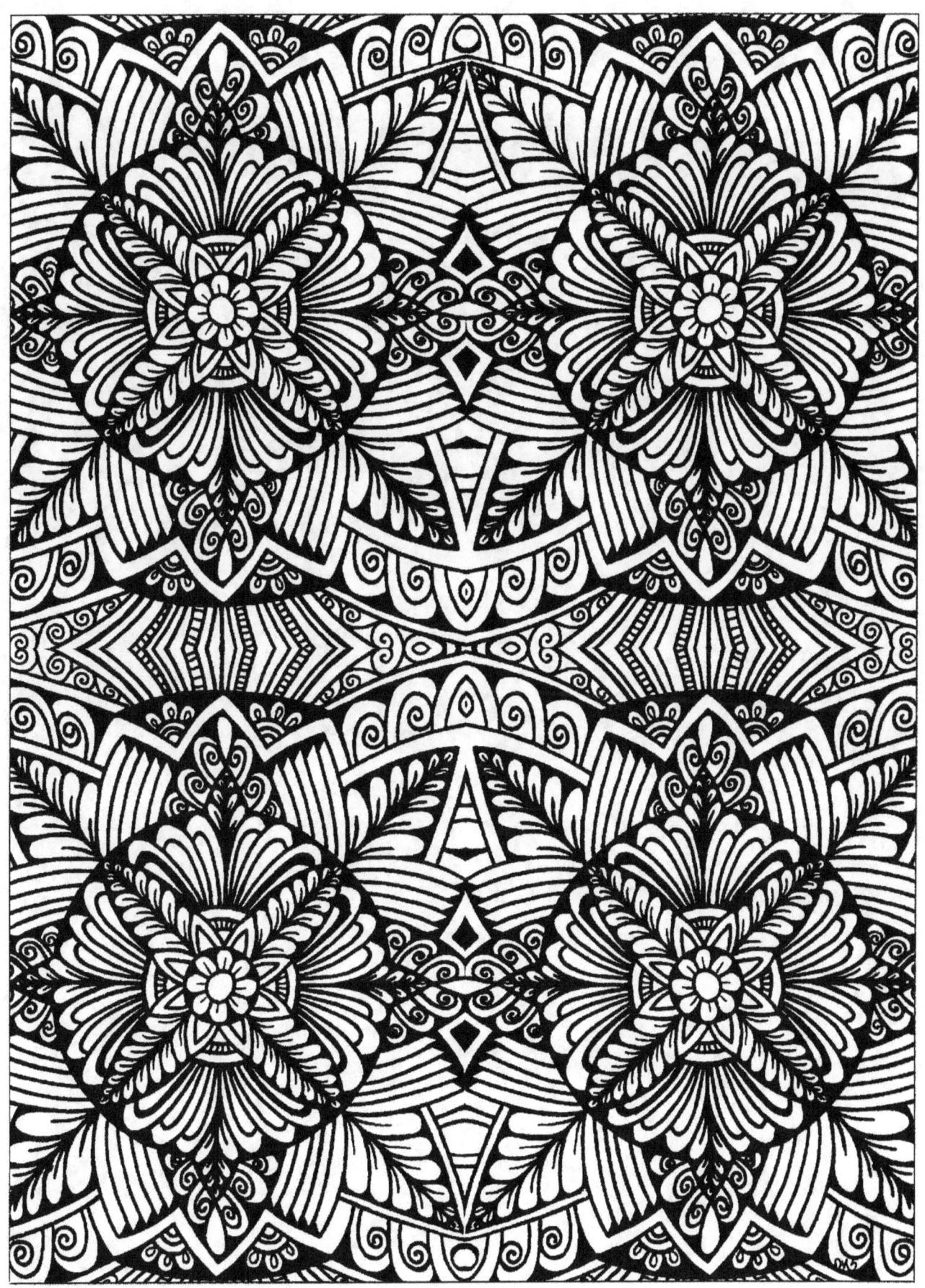

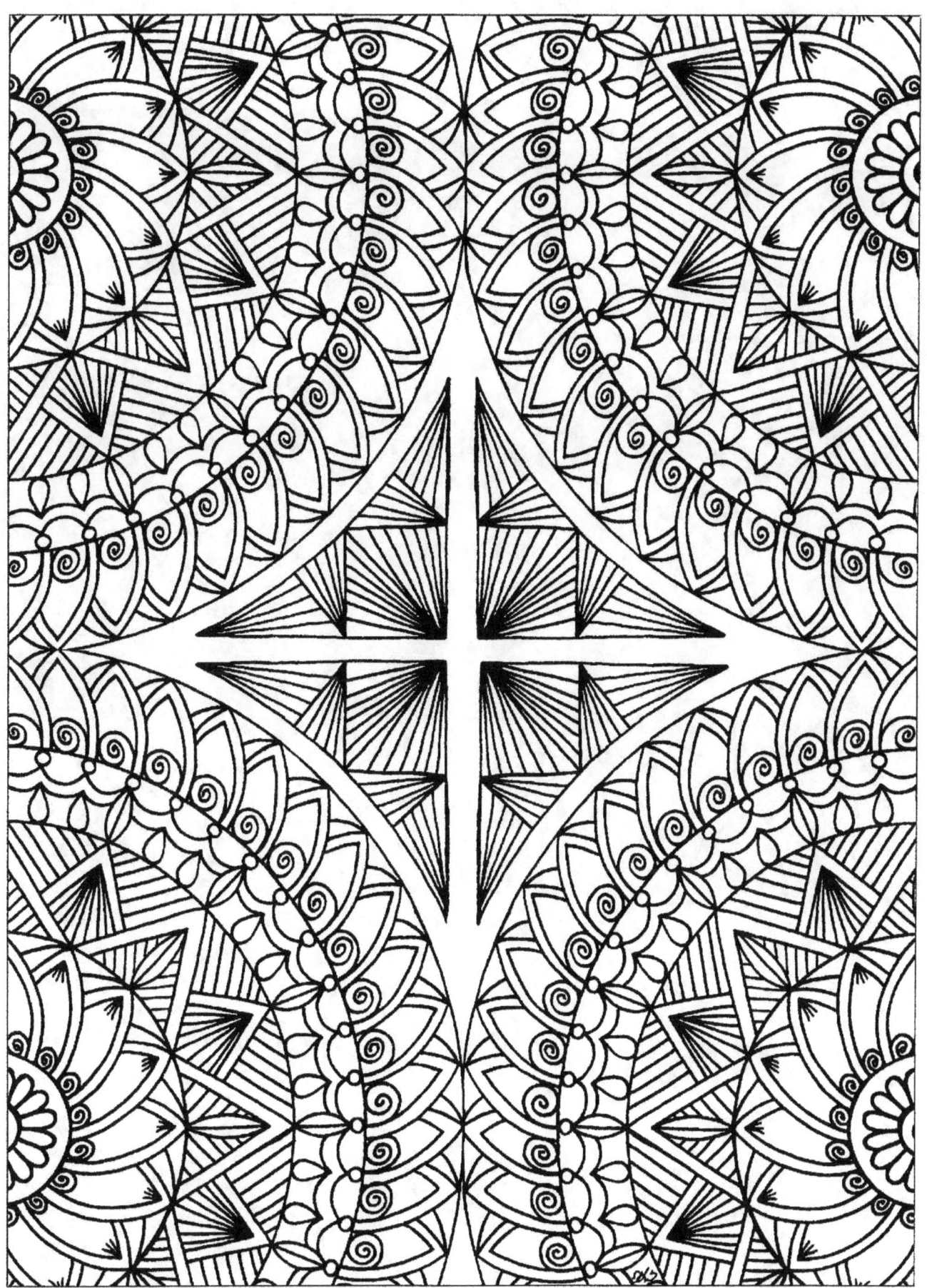

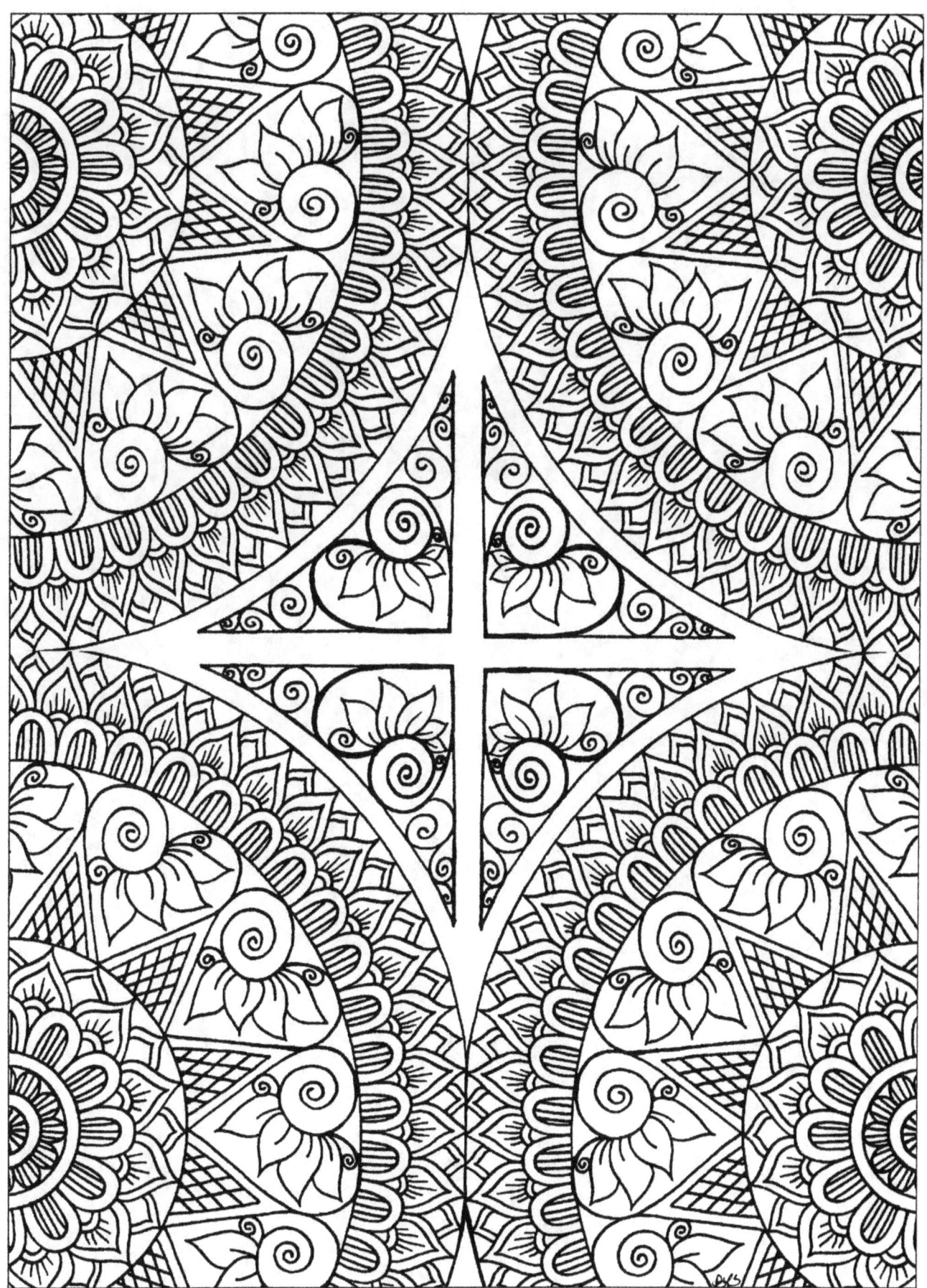

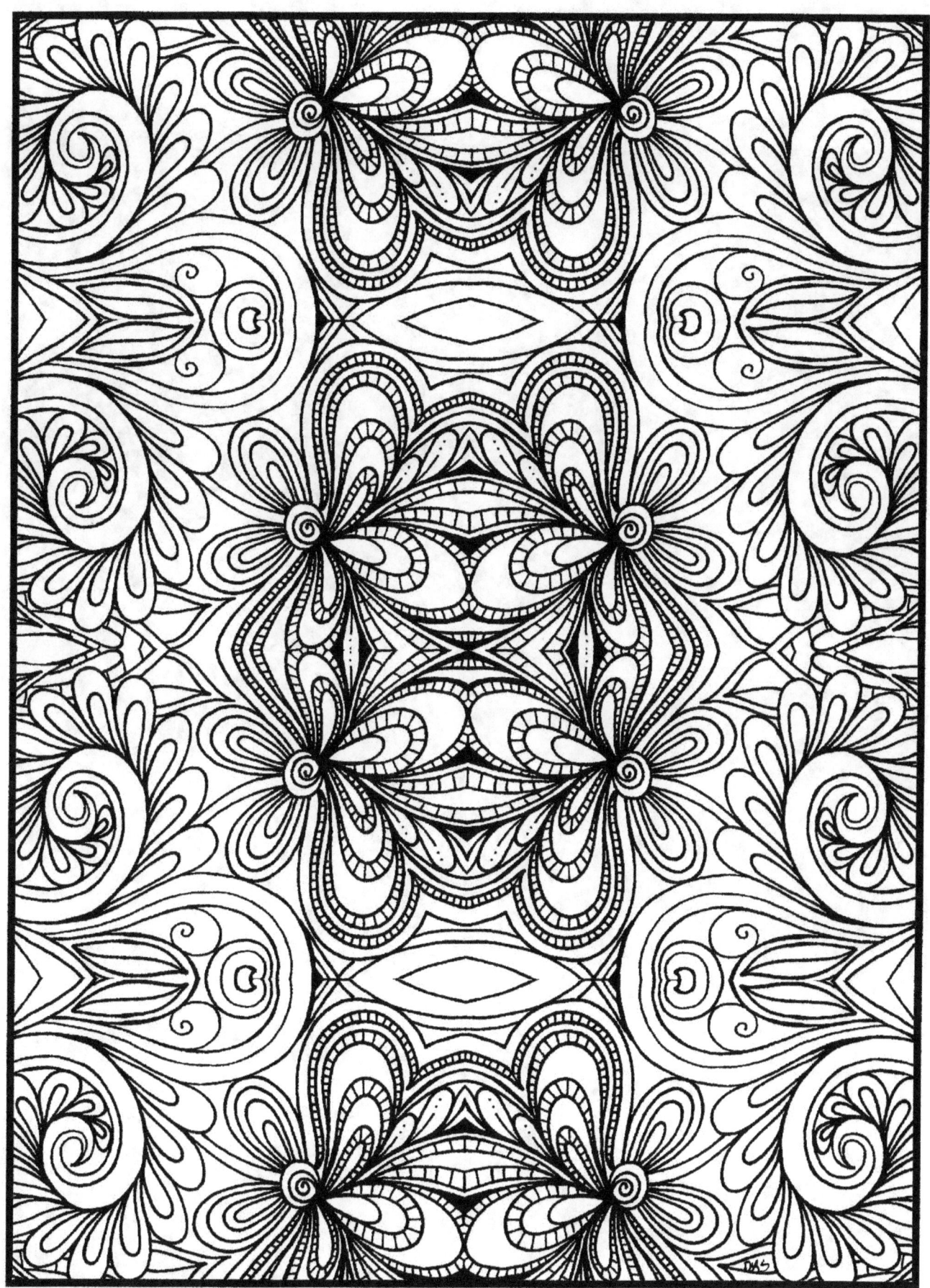

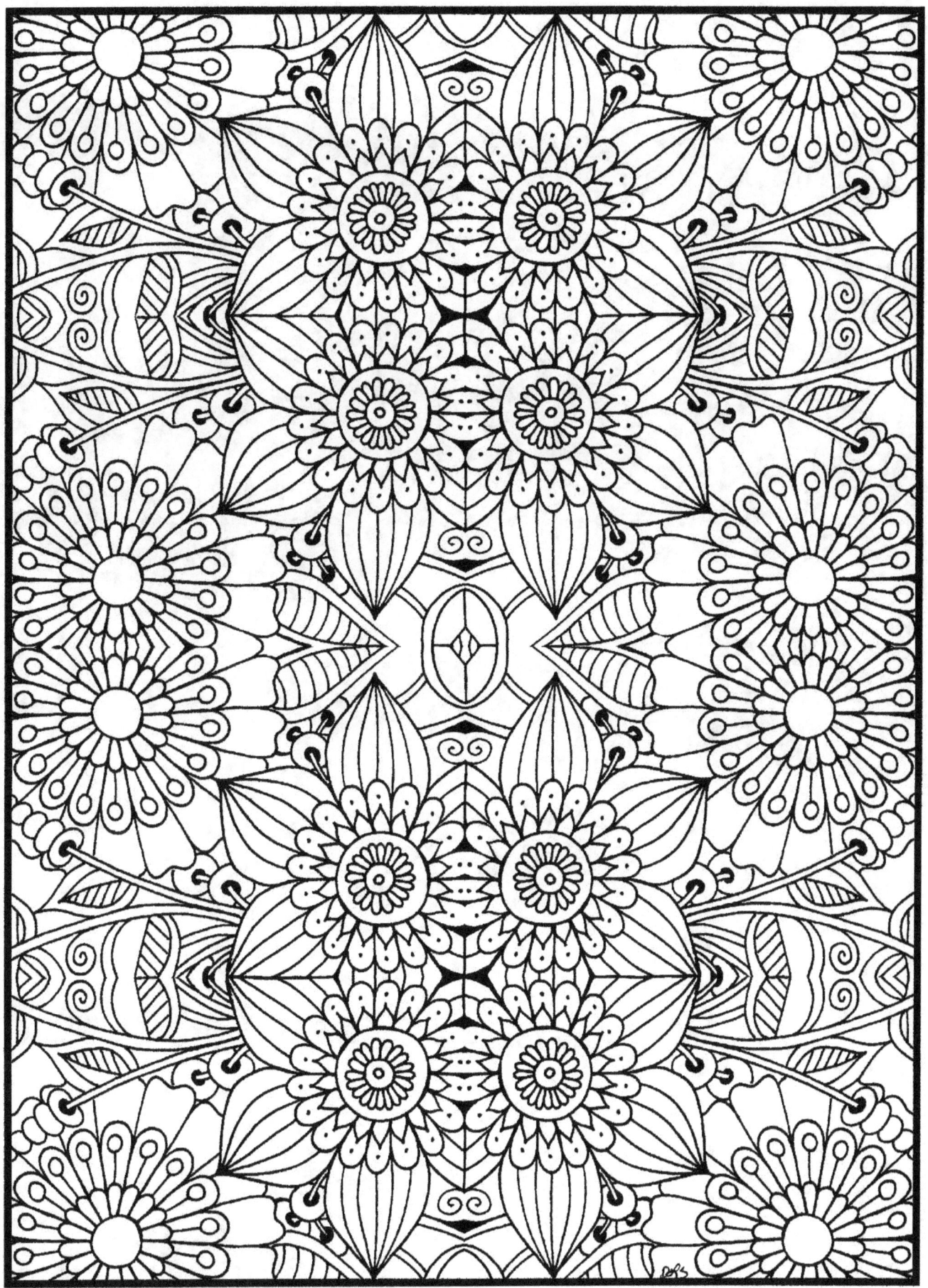

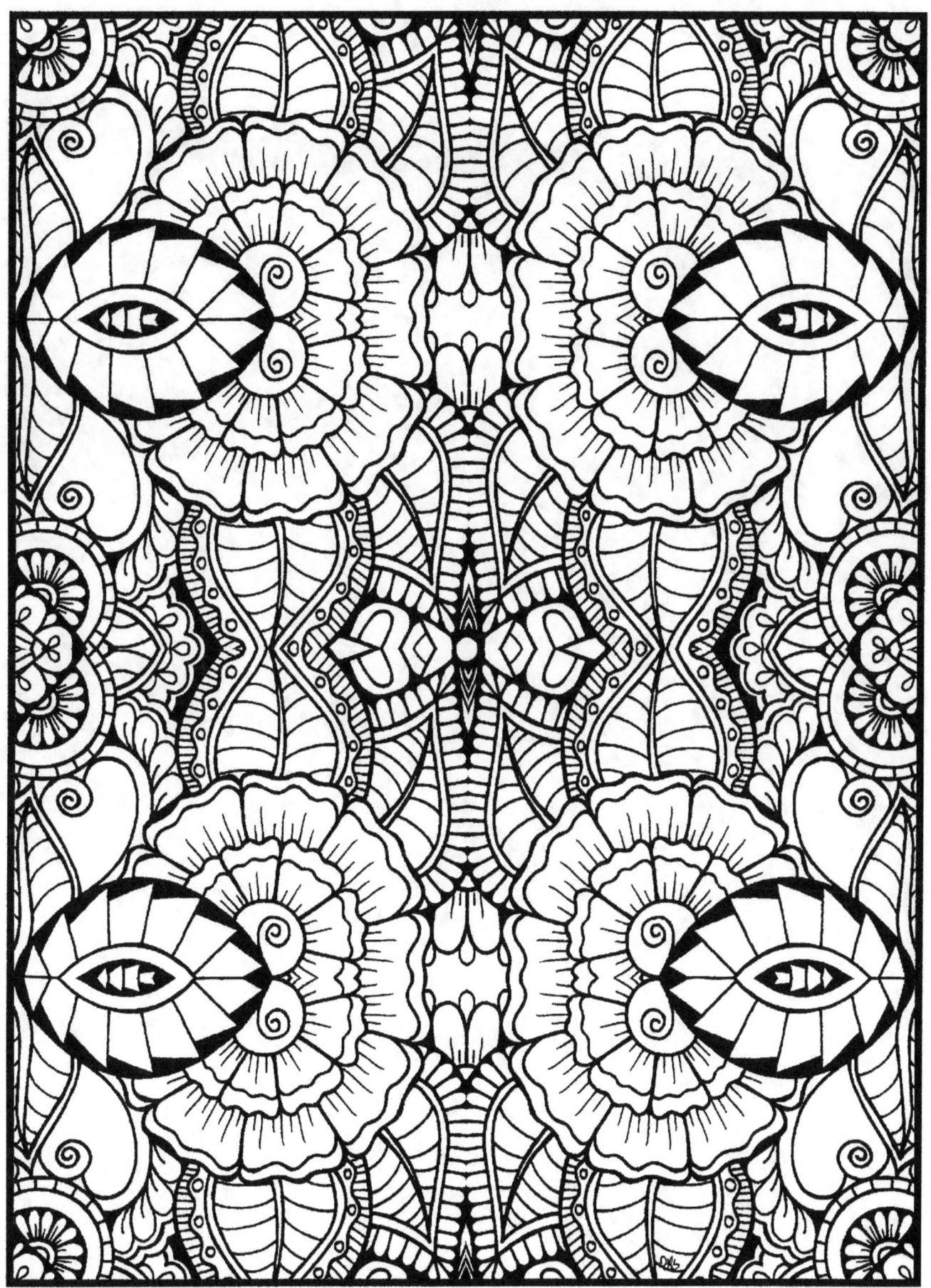

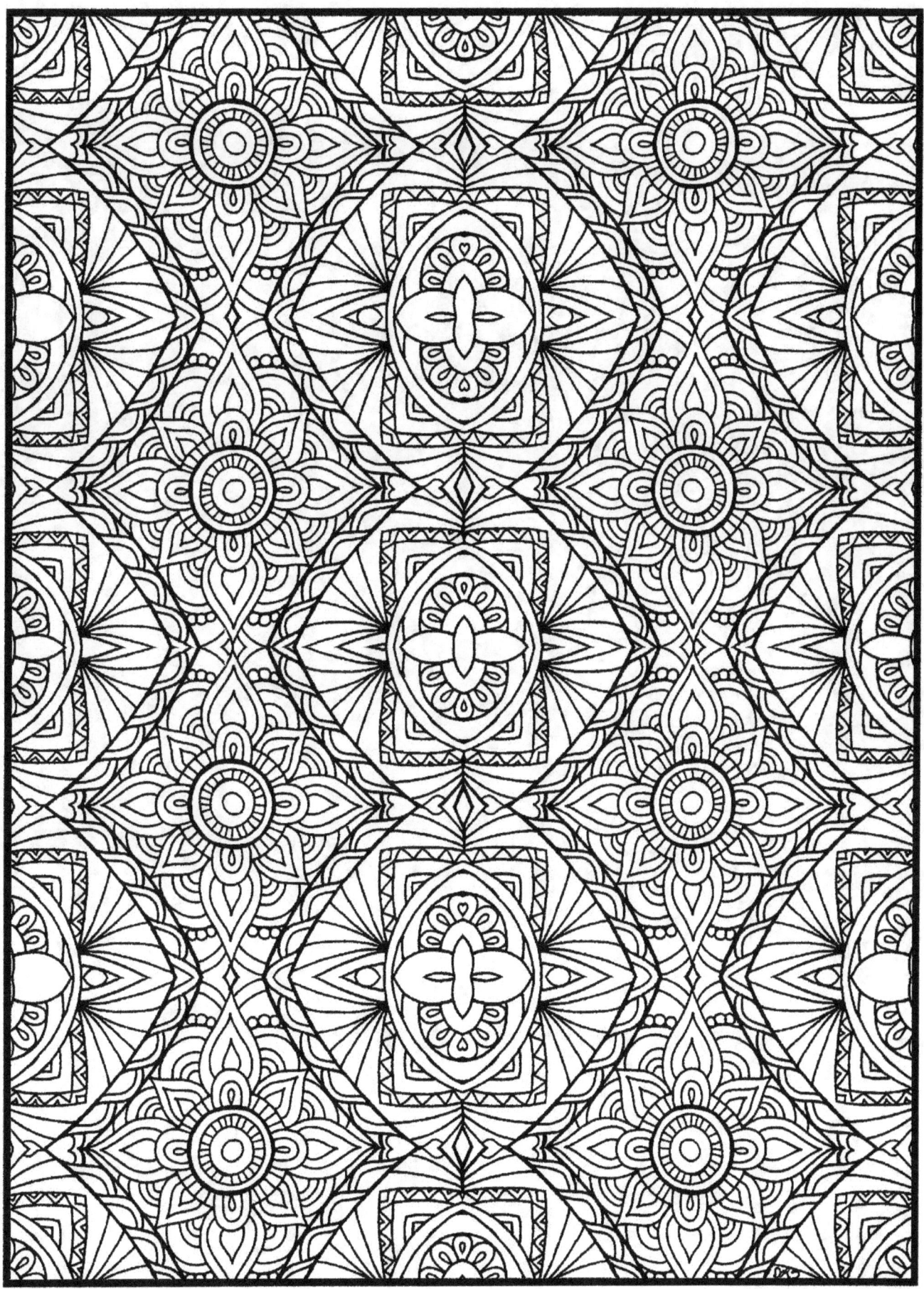

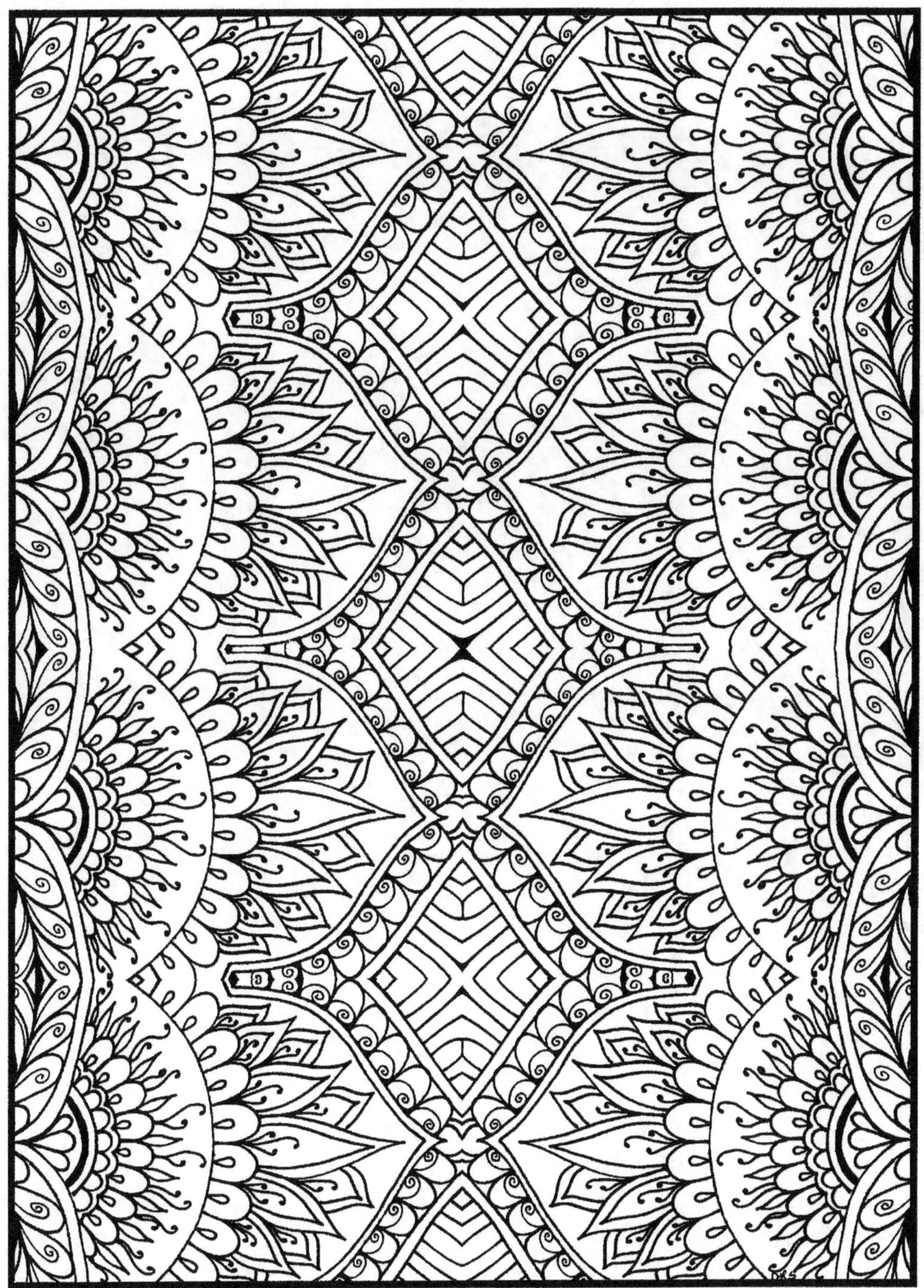

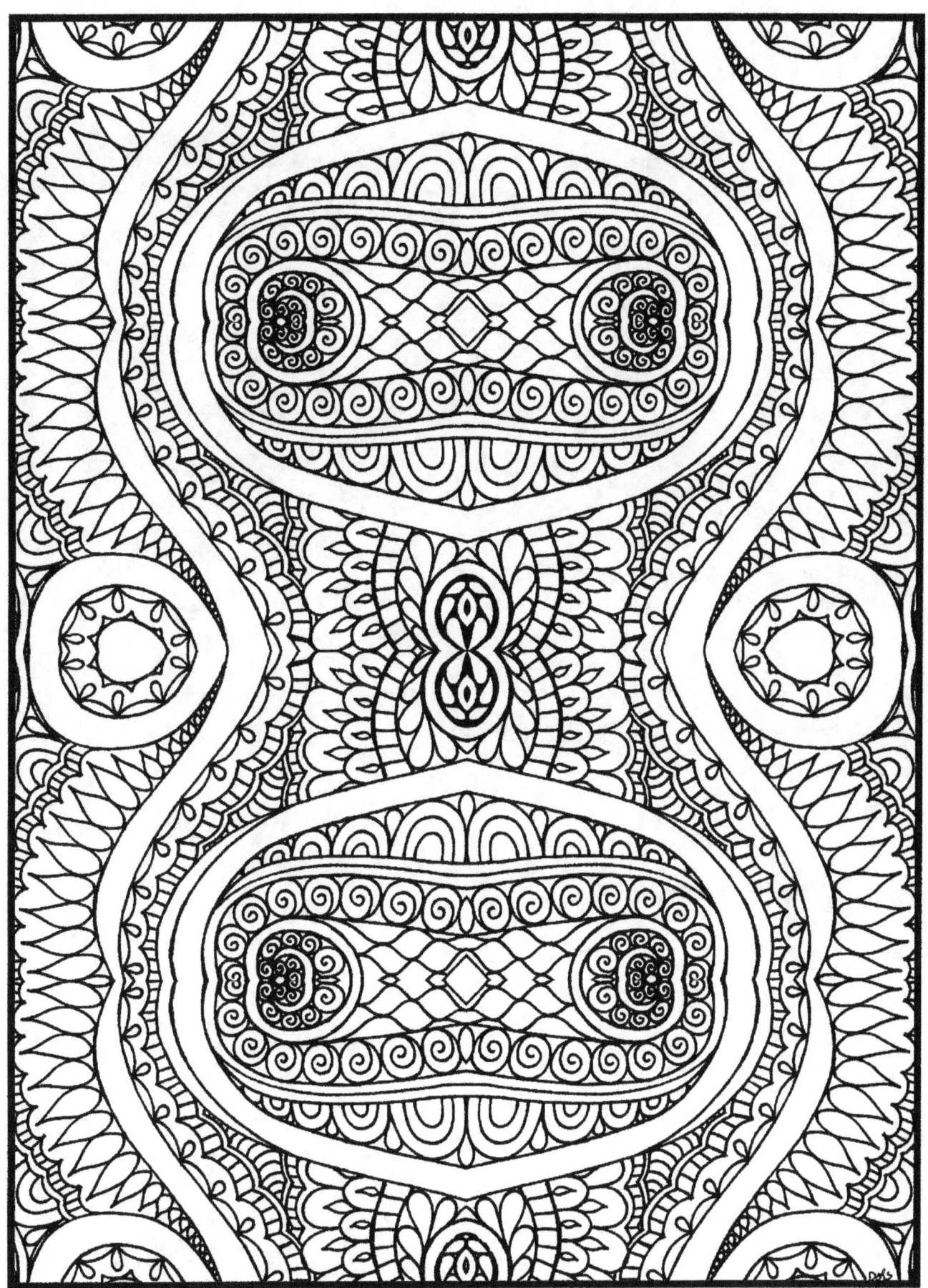

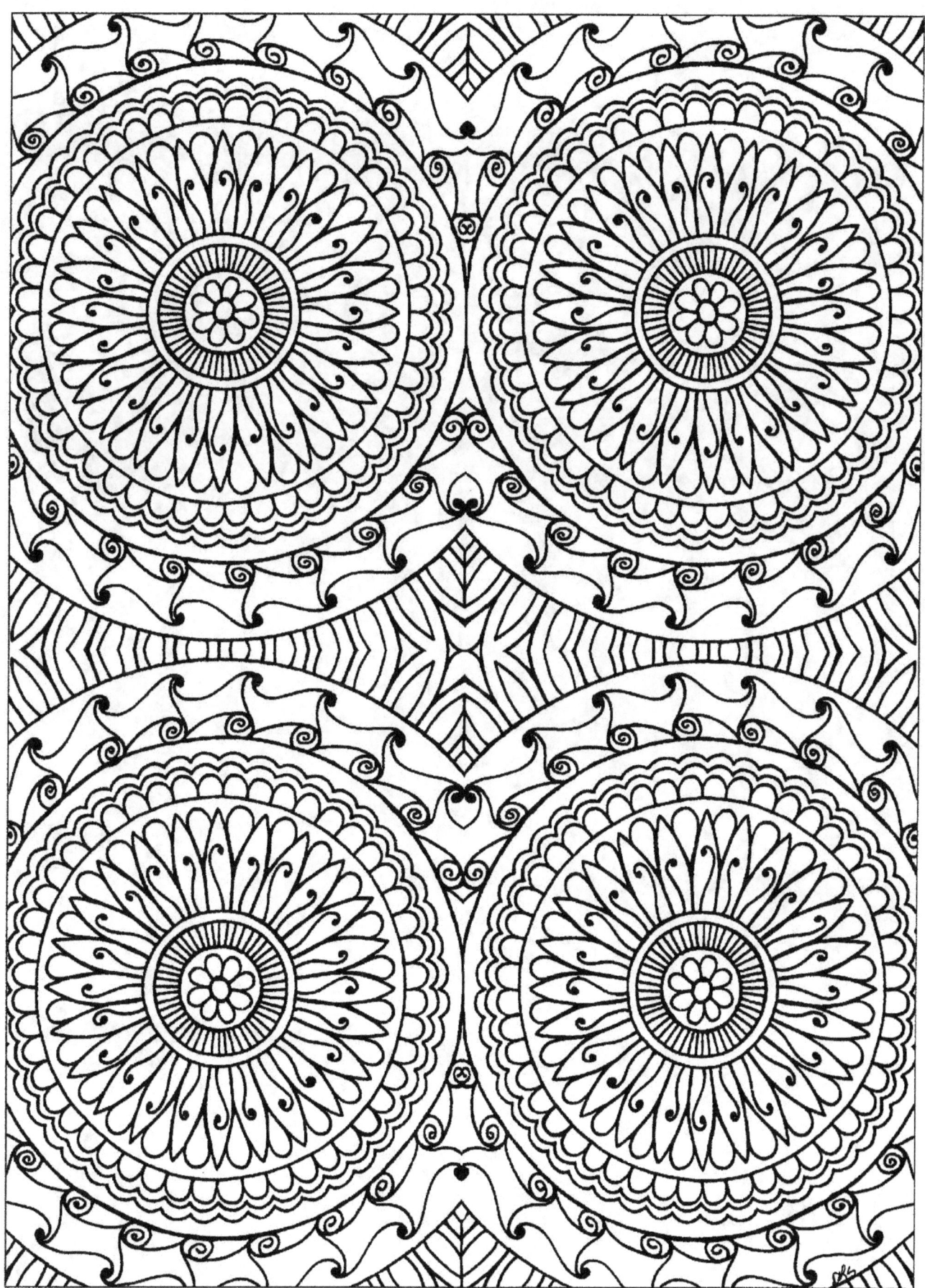

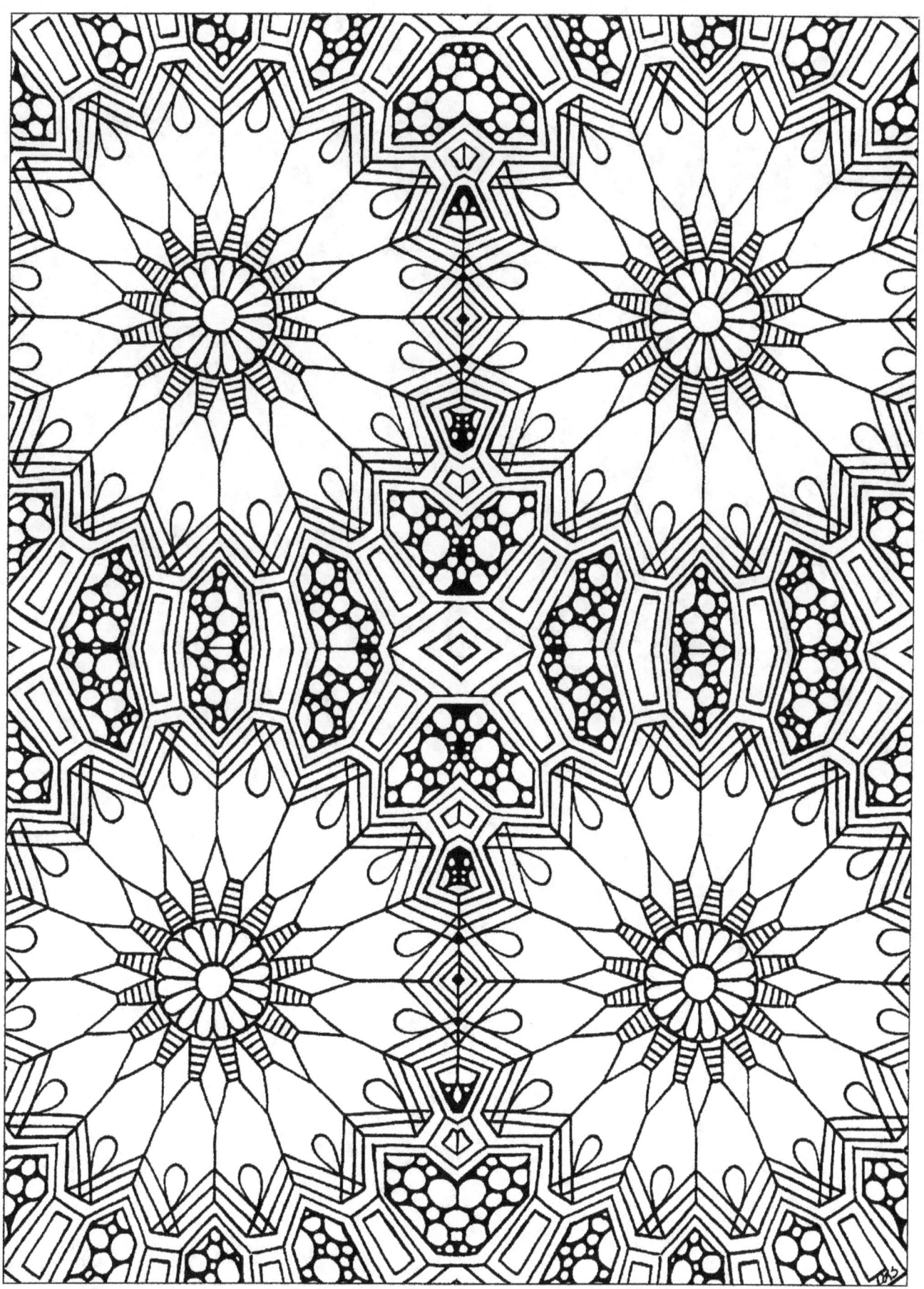

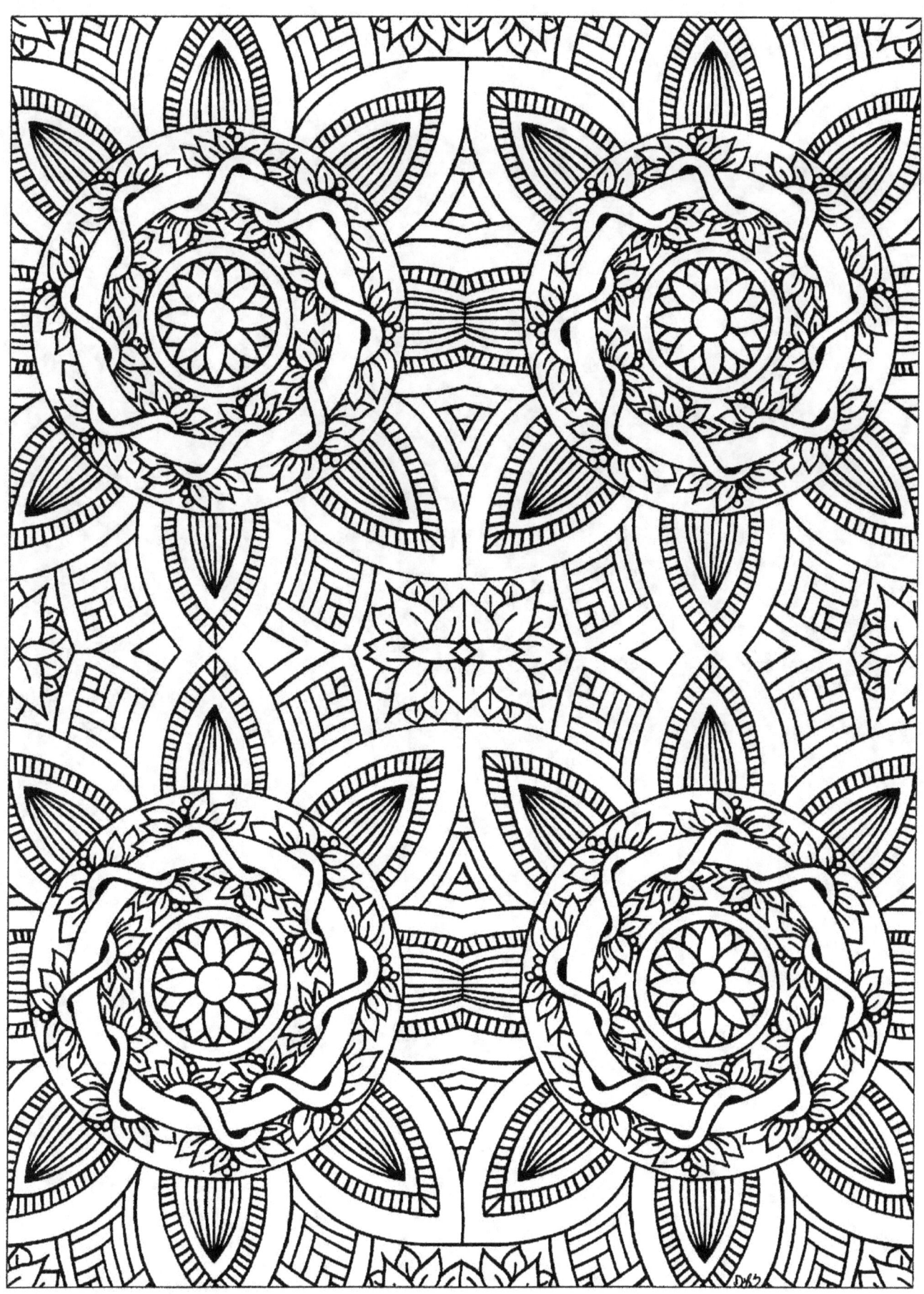

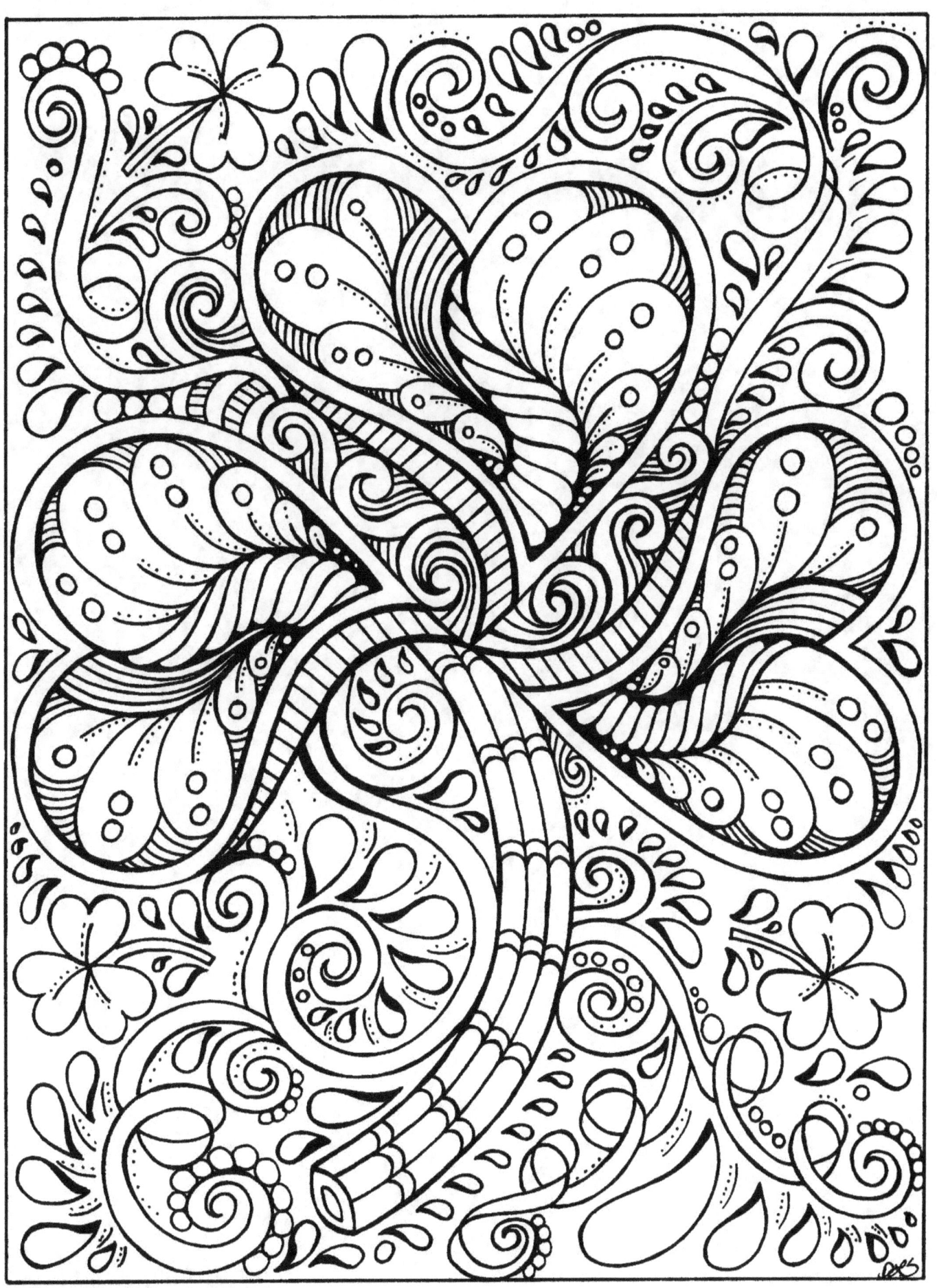

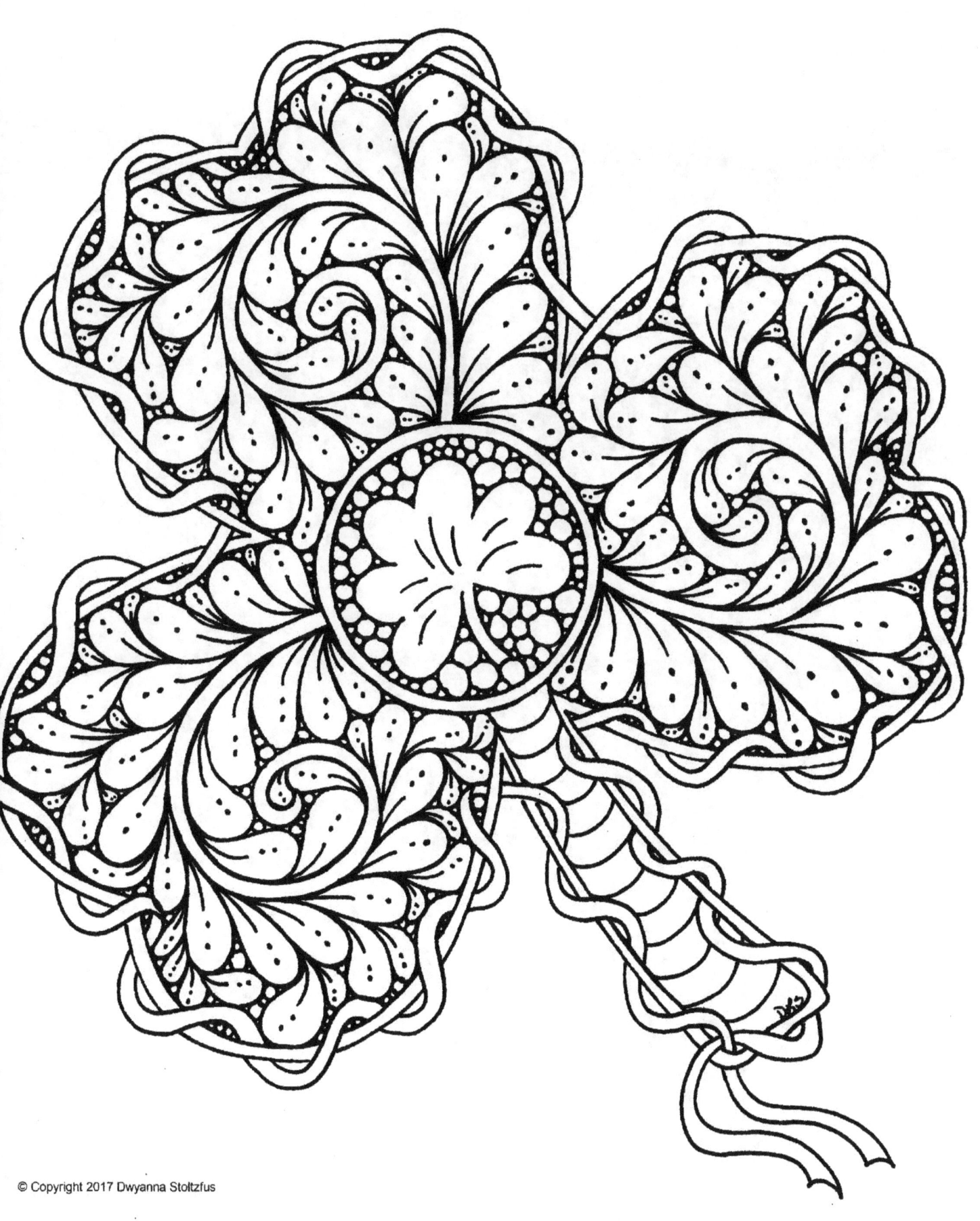

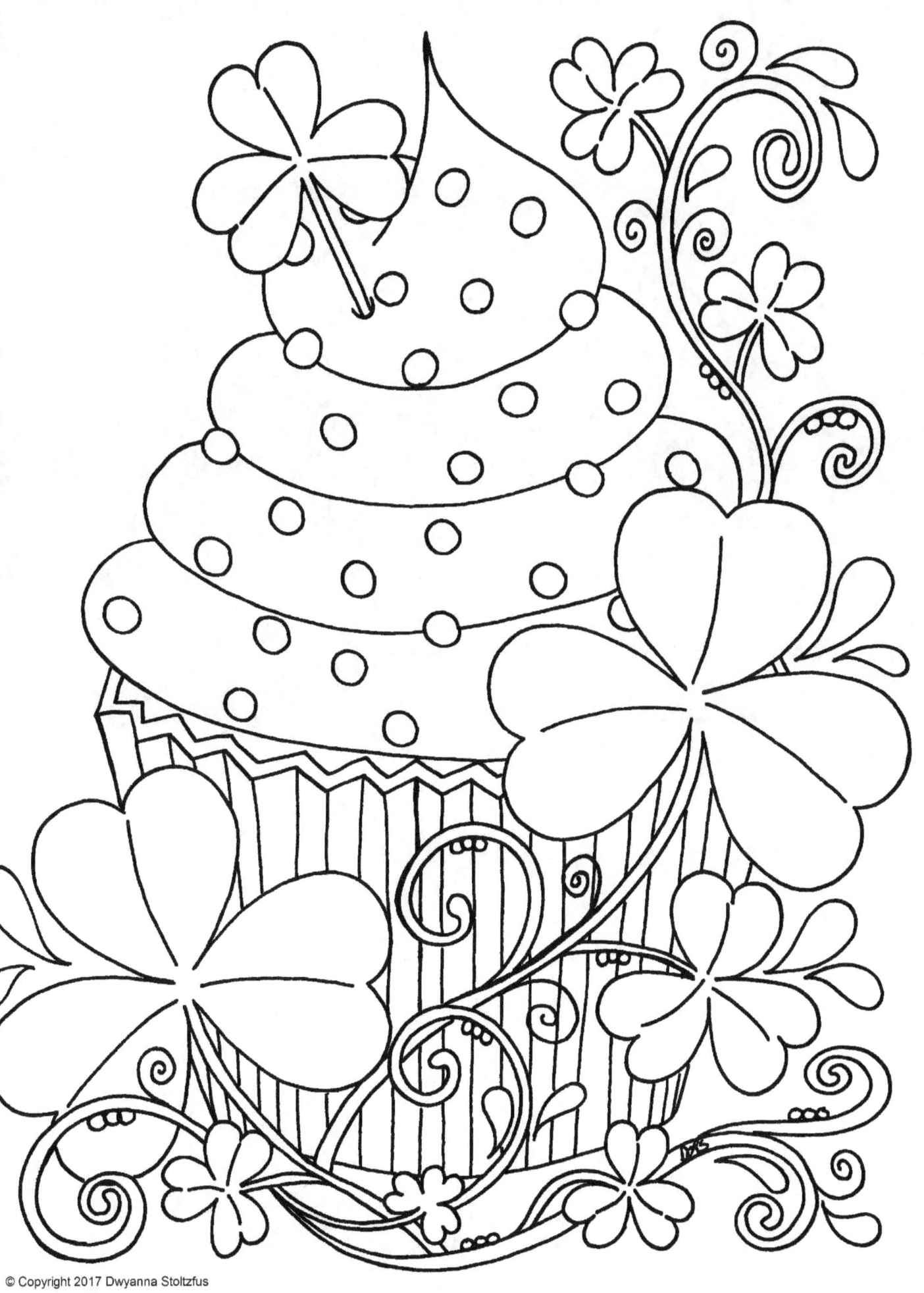

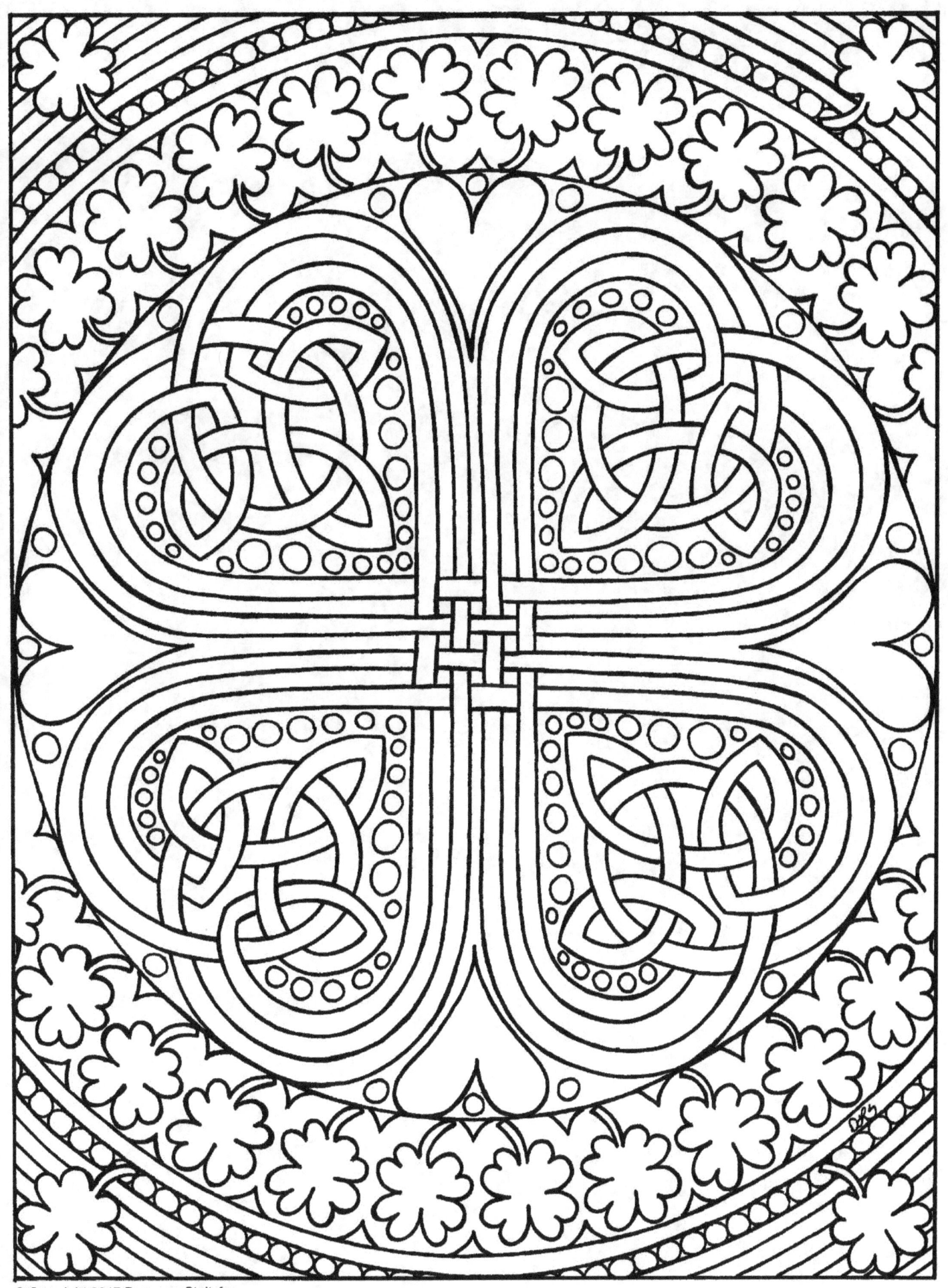

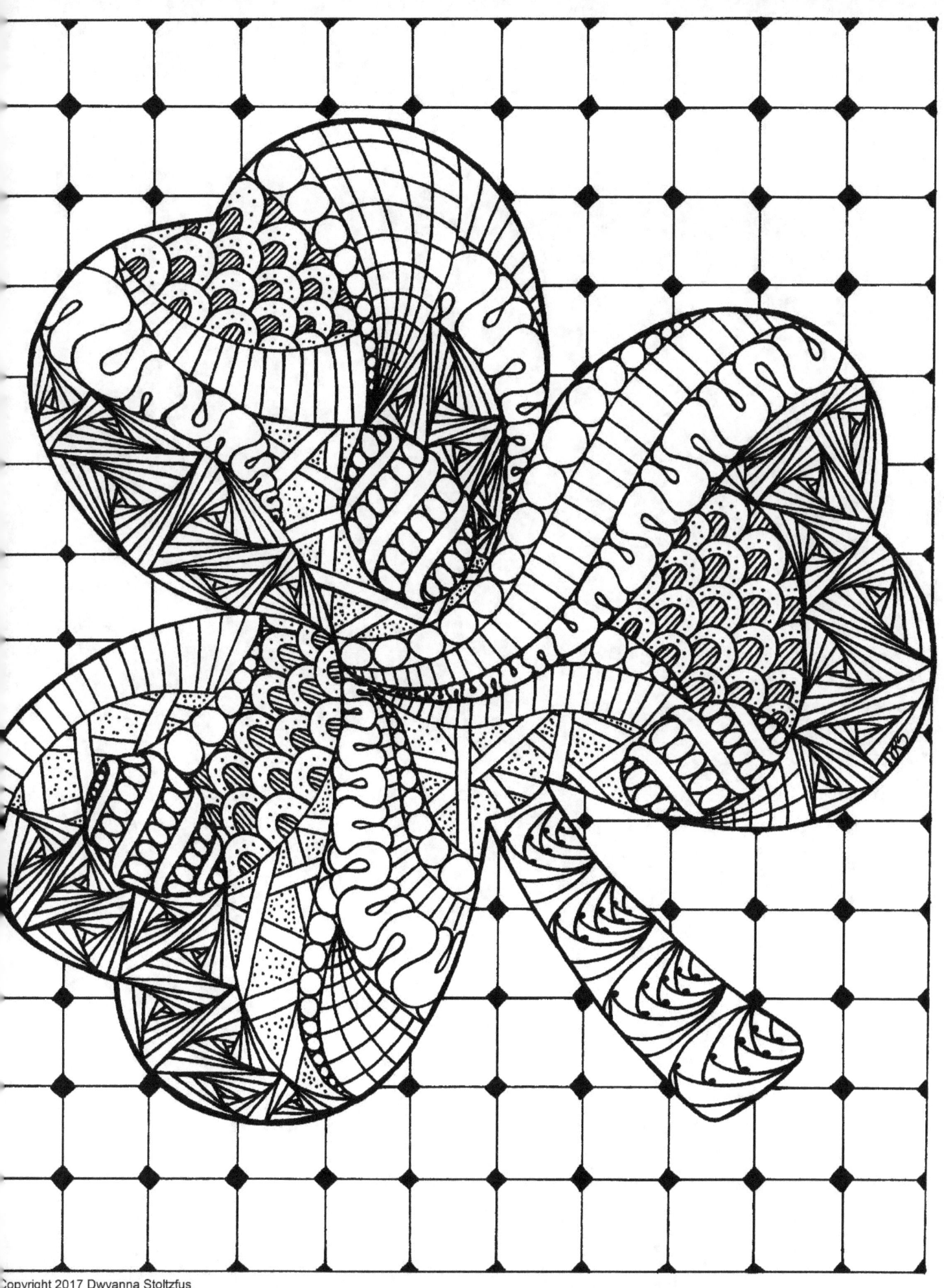

MAY YOUR TROUBLES
✤ BE LESS ✤
and your
Blessings
✤ be MORE ✤
AND NOTHING BUT
HAPPINESS
come through your
door
✤
Irish Blessing

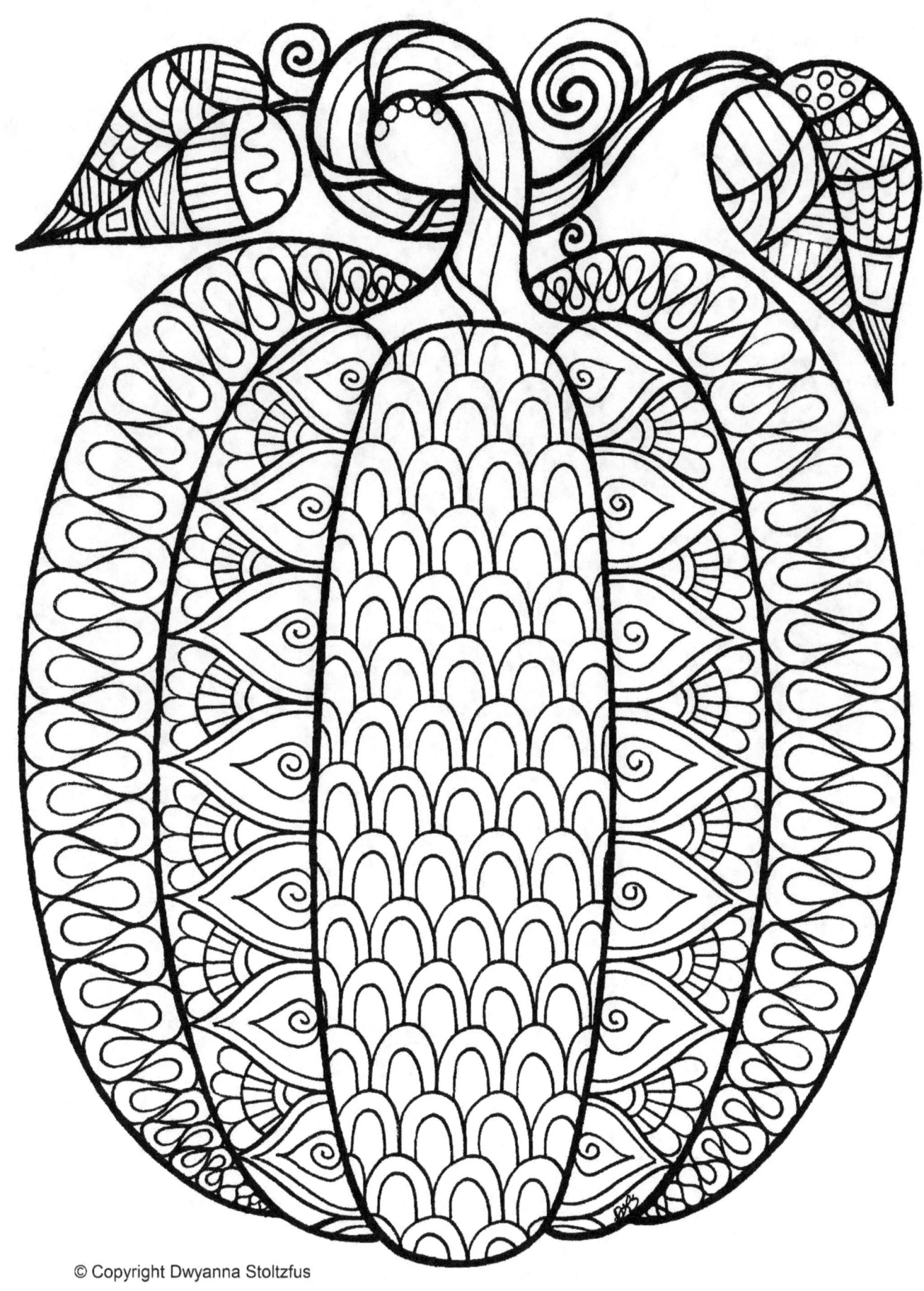

www.ingramcontent.com/pod-product-compliance
Lightning Source LLC
Chambersburg PA
CBHW080836220526
45467CB00008B/2293

*9 781717 386120 *